A Beginner's Guide

to Scientific Method

A Beginner's Guide to Scientific Method

Stephen S. Carey
Portland Community College

Wadsworth Publishing Company
Belmont, California
A Division of Wadsworth, Inc.

Philosophy Editor: *Kenneth King*
Editorial Assistant: *Kristina Pappas*
Production: *Scratchgravel Publishing Services*
Designer: *Michael Rogondino*
Print Buyer: *Barbara Britton*
Permissions Editor: *Robert Kauser*
Copy Editor: *Margaret C. Tropp*
Cover: *Image House*
Compositor: *Scratchgravel Publishing Services*
Printer: *Malloy Lithographing, Inc.*

*This book is printed on
acid-free recycled paper.*

Printed in the United States of America

1 2 3 4 5 6 7 8 9 10—98 97 96 95 94

Library of Congress Cataloging-in-Publication Data

Carey, Stephen S. (Stephen Sayers). 1944–
    A beginner's guide to scientific method / Stephen S. Carey.
        p.   cm.
    Includes bibliographical references and index.
    ISBN 0-534-21126-7 (acid-free paper)
    1. Science—Methodology.   2. Research—Methodology.   I. Title.
Q175.C27 1994
507.2—dc20   93-15423
                                                                     CIP

for the Moose,
but mainly for Leah

Contents

Preface

This book is written for the student who has little or no background in the sciences. Its aim is to provide a brief, nontechnical introduction to the basic methods underlying all good scientific research. Though I use this book as the main text in a college-level critical thinking course for nonscience majors, it could easily be used as a supplement in any course in which students must have some rudimentary understanding of how science is done.

Some will object to the very idea of a basic method underlying all the sciences, on the ground that there is probably nothing all good science has in common other than being judged good science. Although there is certainly something to this objection, there are a few basic procedures to which good scientific research must adhere. If anything deserves to be called *the* scientific method, it is the simple but profoundly fundamental process whereby new ideas are put to the test—everything from the most rarefied and grand theoretical constructs to the experimenter's claims of discovering some new fact about the natural world.

Scientific method rests on the notion that every idea about the workings of nature has consequences and that these consequences provide a basis for testing the idea in question. How this insight is worked out in the world of science is really all this book is about. No doubt much good science is one step removed from the proposing and testing of new ideas, and this is the "something" to the previous objection. But whenever science attempts to understand how or why things happen as they do, a basic, underlying methodology generally emerges. This is not to say that there is a step-by-step recipe which, if followed, will invariably lead to a greater understanding of nature. If this book succeeds at only one thing, I hope it is to show the tentativeness with which scientific results are issued and the utter openness to revision that is essential to good science.

I am a firm believer that to give an account of something is also to account for what it is not. Hence, roughly a third of the text, in parts of Chapter 4 and especially in Chapter 5, is about the antithesis of good science—bogus science or pseudoscience. This material on how *not* to do science is important for the general student because much of the presumed "science" to which he or she will be exposed will be in the rather extravagant claims of the pseudoscientist. To confirm this, one need only look at the astrology column of any major newspaper or turn on one of the many television programs that purport to provide an objective investigation of the paranormal.

I also firmly believe that one generally learns by doing, not by talking about doing. Thus, every important idea in the text is an idea the student will grapple with while solving the chapter exercises. The lengthy set of exercises at the end of each chapter is the part of the book of which I am most proud and for which I can claim some originality. I have tried to write exercises that are challenging and fun to think about, require no special expertise, and yet illustrate the extent to which scientific problem solving requires a great deal of creativity. Many of the exercises come not from the world of official science but from everyday life. My final firm belief is that much of what is involved in attempting to do science is thoroughgoing, hard-working common sense—the very beast instrumental in solving many of the problems of our day-to-day lives.

Note also two additional features of the exercises. First, for the most part, chapter exercises are written in a manner that requires the student to work with a number of key ideas all at once. At the end of Chapter 2, for example, the student is asked to think about six issues, some of which involve subissues, for each exercise. (Indeed, the exercise instructions are longer than any single exercise!) This introduces students straightaway to the fact that most interesting problems involve a complex of issues and problem solving begins with two essential steps: (1) getting a good overall sense of the problem or problems and (2) only then beginning to break its solution down into a series of discrete bits of critical work. However, the exercises are designed in such a way that individual tasks can be worked on in relative isolation from one another. Thus, for example, the first task the student is asked to complete for each of the problems at the end of Chapter 2 is "state the facts to be explained and the proposed explanation." This task can easily be discussed separately and with reference to each of the exercises.

Second, several of the exercise sets, particularly those at the end of Chapters 2 and 3, contain many exercises that may seem to be redundant. I do not require my students to do all exercises. Rather, I pick a few exercises to use in class for purposes of illustration and assign a few to be done as homework and then discussed in class. Still others I hold in reserve to deal with particular points that require further discussion, depending on the responses and questions of my students.

The first several exercises in Chapters 2 through 4 all require the students to design some sort of experiment. I have found these exercises particularly useful in encouraging students to think both creatively and critically. I assign different problems to small groups of students as homework to be done as a group. The homework results of each group are then exchanged with another group who must criticize the experiment design. In class, designers and criticizers meet and refine each of the two experiments on which they have been working. My role in the process is largely to keep the troops calm and to mediate any potentially explosive disputes.

Pedagogical demands aside, the appearance of redundancy in the long exercise sets is somewhat superficial. Although students are asked to do a few things over and over, they must think about very different things in each problem. The contribution of generalized strategies to problem solving—in science and in most other areas of our lives as well—is significant but not of overriding importance. To solve a problem about X, one may be aided by a general sense of how such problems are solved, but one absolutely must know a good deal about X. Thus, the unique considerations—the details—that necessarily intrude in the solution of each problem make that problem worth considering despite the fact that its solution may involve a well-worn strategy. The "devil" really is in the details, as can be seen in the sample solutions provided for certain exercises in each chapter.

Haven taken much credit for innovation in the chapter exercises, I can claim little originality for much of the expository material, particularly in the first three chapters of this book. The case study at the center of Chapter 1 will reveal, to those familiar with the philosophy of science, my indebtedness to the work of Carl Hempel, particularly his classic introductory text, *The Philosophy of Natural Science*. The central approach and organization of Chapter 3 owes much to Ronald Giere's excellent text, *Understanding Scientific Reasoning*. I also had the good fortune to receive the advice of several readers of earlier versions of my manuscript, including Davis Baird, University of South Carolina; Stanley Baronett and Todd Jones, University of Nevada, Las Vegas; Brad Dowden, California State University, Sacramento; Jim Kalat, North Carolina State University; and Bonnie Paller, California State University, Northridge.

One final note. Though my field is philosophy, conspicuously missing in this text is any emphasis on central topics in the philosophy of science. There is, for example, no explicit discussion of the hypothetical-deductive method, of the covering law model of explanation, nor of their attendant difficulties, of the rather more notorious problems in the theory of confirmation, nor of the infighting between realists and antirealists. My hunch (which is considerably less than a firm belief) is that an introduction to anything should avoid philosophical contemplation about the foundations of that thing, lest it lose focus, if not its course, in the sight of its audience. Once the thing in question is fully absorbed and understood, then and only then is the time for philosophical contemplation of its deep commitments.

Though I have not altogether avoided topics dear to the philosopher of science, I discuss them briefly and, for the most part, in a jargon-free fashion. My hope is that I have not purchased economy and readability at the expense of either accuracy or a sense of wonder about the philosophical issues embedded in the methods by which science is conducted.

Stephen S. Carey

A Beginner's Guide

to Scientific Method

1

Science

Science when well digested is nothing but good sense and reason.
—Stanislaus, *Maxims* (No. 43)

Just What Is Science?

We all have a passing familiarity with the world of science. Rarely does a week go by without a new scientific study or discovery being reported in the media. "Astronomers confirm space structure that's mind-boggling in its immensity" and "Scientists identify gene tied to alcoholism" are the headlines from two recent stories in my daily newspaper. Yet many of us would be hard-pressed to say much more about the nature of science than that science is whatever it is scientists do for a living. Hardly an illuminating definition!

So, what more might we say in response to the question "Just what is science?" We cannot hope to answer this question by looking at the subject matter of the sciences. Science investigates natural phenomena of every conceivable sort—from the physical to the biological to the social. Scientists study everything from events occurring at the time of the formation of the universe to the stages of human intellectual and emotional development to the migratory patterns of butterflies. Judging by its subject matter, then, science is the study of very nearly everything.

Nor can we hope to answer our question by looking at the range of activities in which scientists engage. Scientists theorize about things, organize vast research projects, build equipment, dig up relics, take polls, run experiments on everything from people to protons to plants; the list is almost endless. A description of science in terms of the sorts of things scientists typically do, then, is not going to tell us much about the nature of science, for there does not seem to be anything scientists typically do.

If we are to understand just what science is, we must look at science from a different perspective. We must ask ourselves, first, why scientists study the natural world. And next, we must look to the way in which scientific inquiry is conducted, no matter what its subject.

Asking Why

Of course, we cannot hope to give a simple, ubiquitous reason why each and every scientist studies the natural world. There are bound to be as many reasons as there are practicing scientists. Nevertheless, there is a single "why" underlying all scientific research. In general, scientists study the natural world to figure out *why* things happen as they do. We all know, for example, that the moon is riddled with craters. From a scientific point of view, what is of interest is precisely why this should be so. What natural processes have led to the formation of the craters? Thus, part of the answer to our question "Just what is science?" is the following: *Science is that activity whose underlying aim is to further our understanding of why things happen as they do in the world in which we live.* To see what it is that scientists actually do in attempting to "make sense" of nature, let's take a look at an historical instance that, as it turns out, played an important role in the development of modern medicine.

Up until the middle of the 19th century, little was known about the nature of infectious diseases and the ways in which they are transmitted. In the mid-1800s, however, an important clue emerged from the work of a Viennese doctor, Ignaz Semmelweis. At the time, many pregnant women who entered Vienna General Hospital died shortly after giving birth. Their deaths were attributed to something called "childbed fever." Curiously, the death rate from childbed fever in the hospital ward where the patients were treated by physicians was five times higher than in another ward where women were seen only by midwives. Physicians were at a loss to explain why this should be so. But then something remarkable occurred. One of Semmelweis's colleagues cut his finger on a scalpel that had been used during an autopsy. Within days, the colleague exhibited symptoms remarkably like those associated with childbed fever, and subsequently he died. Semmelweis knew that physicians often spent time with students in the autopsy room prior to visiting their patients in the maternity ward.

Now, the phenomenon that Semmelweis wanted to understand is clear: the remarkable difference in the death rates from childbed fever in the two wards. Relying largely on the clue provided by the death of his colleague, Semmelweis speculated that something like the following might be responsible for the difference in death rates: Perhaps childbed fever is caused by something that physicians come into contact with in the autopsy room and then inadvertently transmit to pregnant women during the course of their rounds in the maternity ward. This something Semmelweis appropriately termed "cadaveric matter."

Offering Explanations

In effect, Semmelweis told what we might call an *explanatory story*. The story Semmelweis told has two distinct elements. First are the facts that puzzled him—notably, the marked difference in rates of death by childbed fever in the two wards and the fact that physicians attended patients only in the ward where the death rate was higher. The second element in the story is a set of purely conjectural factors that would, if true, account for those puzzling facts. The conjectural factors in Semmelweis's story are the claims that something in cadaveric matter causes childbed fever and that this something can be transmitted from cadaver to physician to patient by simple bodily contact.

As our example suggests, the first step in making sense of some part of the natural world is to tell an explanatory story—a story that, if true, would explain whatever it is we are trying to understand. Semmelweis's explanatory story is all the more interesting because it introduced what were, at the time, some very new and controversial ideas about the way in which disease is transmitted. Many of Semmelweis's contemporaries believed that childbed fever was the result of an epidemic, like the black plague, that somehow infected only pregnant women. Others suspected that dietary problems or difficulties in the general care of the women were to blame. In telling his explanatory story, Semmelweis hinted at the existence of a new set of explanatory factors that challenged the best explanations of the day and had the potential to advance dramatically current views about how diseases are spread.

Explanatory stories need not involve such controversial new notions, however. Indeed, in our daily lives we often work with explanatory stories of a more mundane sort. Imagine, for example, the following case. For the past few nights, you haven't been sleeping well. You've had a hard time getting to sleep and have begun waking up frequently during the night. This is unusual, for you are normally a sound sleeper. What could be causing the problem? Well, next week is final exam week, and you've been staying up late every evening, studying. Could concern about your upcoming exams be causing the problem? This seems unlikely, since you've been through exam week several times before and haven't had any problems sleeping. Is there anything else unusual about your behavior the past few nights? It has been quite warm, so you have been consuming large quantities of your favorite drink, iced tea. This could explain the problem. You are well aware that most teas, like coffee, contain a stimulant, caffeine, though tea usually contains much less than coffee. It may well be the caffeine in the iced tea that is disturbing your sleep.

Though nothing of any great scientific consequence turns on the solution of our little puzzle, the way in which we have undertaken its solution nonetheless involves precisely the elements we identified in Semmelweis's work on childbed fever. The puzzling fact here is your recent inability to sleep soundly. The key factors in the explanatory story are your increased iced tea consumption and the fact that iced tea contains a stimulant. Thus, to a large extent, thinking about things from a scientific perspective—thinking about the "hows" and "whys" of things—involves thinking in ways with which you are already familiar.

These two cases—the scientific and the mundane—have something else in common. Both provide us with explanations of something puzzling, yet in neither case do we have any tangible evidence that the explanation offered is correct. No doubt, if there is something in cadaveric matter that can cause childbed fever, then Semmelweis's explanation might be on the right track. Similarly, it may be the iced tea that is causing your sleeplessness. But then again, it may be something else, something we have not yet considered; it may even be a combination of the iced tea and other factors. Earlier, we observed that science aims at explaining natural phenomena. Now we need to look at the way in which proposed explanations are put to the test. Not coincidentally, the second part of the answer to our question "Just what is science?" involves the way in which explanatory stories are tested, both in the world of official science and in our daily lives.

Testing Explanations

Consider once again our problem of sleeplessness. You have a hunch that your recent inability to sleep is a result of your increased consumption of caffeine. But is this the right explanation? In this instance, a relatively quick, easy, and effective test can be performed. You might, for example, try drinking ice water instead of iced tea in the evening. If you were to do this, and if you began sleeping normally again, we would have good reason to think that our explanation is correct: It must be the caffeine in the iced tea. Conversely, if you did not begin sleeping normally, we would have some reason to suspect that we have not yet found the right explanation: Eliminating the caffeine didn't seem to do the trick.

At the heart of our proposed test lies the following strategy: First, we looked for a consequence of our explanatory story—something that ought to occur if circumstances are properly arranged and if our story is on the right track. If caffeine is causing your sleeplessness, and if we arrange for you to stop consuming caffeine, we would expect your sleeplessness to stop. Next, we took pains to arrange these circumstances: We stopped your caffeine consumption. Finally, we waited to see what would happen—whether or not the predicted result would actually occur.

Something very much like this same strategy was employed by Semmelweis in testing his explanatory story. Semmelweis reasoned as follows: If childbed fever is caused by cadaveric matter transmitted from physician to patient, and if something were done to eradicate all traces of cadaveric matter from the physicians prior to their visiting patients in the maternity ward, then the incidence of childbed fever should diminish. In fact, Semmelweis arranged for physicians to wash their hands and arms in chlorinated lime water—a powerful cleansing agent—prior to their rounds in the maternity ward. Within two years, the death rate from childbed fever in the ward attended by physicians approached that of the ward attended by midwives. By 1848, Semmelweis was losing not a single woman to childbed fever!

It is this experimental strategy that provides the second part of the answer to our question "Just what is science?" Science is characterized by its underlying interest in making sense of things. It does so, first, by proposing explanations for natural phenomena and, second, by devising experimental conditions under which explanations can be tested. And as we have seen, the experimental strategy on which scientists rely is not all that different from the kind of commonsense strategy we ourselves follow in answering the "hows" and "whys" of our daily lives.

Scientific Method

You may have noticed that the title of this book is *A Beginner's Guide to Scientific Method*, not *A Beginner's Guide to Science*. What, you may ask, is this thing called scientific method? If by *scientific method* we mean something like a step-by-step recipe generally followed by scientists in their research, our answer will have to be that there is no single scientific method. Our discussion earlier of the broad variety of scientific interests and activities certainly bears this out. But a common thread runs through all good scientific research: adherence to the experimental strategy we have been discussing, along with a set of basic standards for judging the merits of experiments designed to test explanations. It is this strategy that we can roughly but accurately describe as the basic method of the sciences. In a nutshell, then, we can say that *scientific method is a rigorous process whereby new ideas about how some part of the natural world works are put to the test.*

In the chapters that follow, we will need to add a great deal of detail to our initial sketch of scientific method. We will also come to recognize that scientific method is not all that straightforward nor, for that matter, easy to apply. Explanations are not always as readily tested as our initial examples might suggest, nor are test results always as decisive as we might like them to be. We will also find that, with some minor variations, scientific method can be used to test things other than explanations. But when all is said and done, when we have followed the rather intricate twists and turns involved in applying scientific method, we will have at our disposal an accurate picture of the basic methodology underlying scientific research.

Before moving on, an important caveat is in order. In focusing on the preoccupation of science with making sense of nature by providing and testing explanations, we have ignored what is surely an equally compelling interest of the sciences—namely, making the world a better place to live through technological innovation. Indeed, when we think of science, we often think of it in terms of some of its more spectacular applications: computers, high-speed trains and jets, nuclear reactors, microwave ovens, new vaccines, and so on. Yet our account of what is involved in science is principally an account of science at the theoretical level, not at the level of application to technological problems.

Don't be misled by our use of the term *theoretical*. Theories are often thought of as little more than guesses or hunches about things. In this everyday sense, if we have a theory about something, we have at most a kind of baseless conjecture about it. In science, however, *theory* has a related but different meaning. Scientific theories may be tentative and, at a certain point in their development, will involve a fair amount of guesswork. But what makes a scientific theory a *theory* is its ability to explain—not the fact that at some point in its development it may contain some rather questionable notions. Just as there will be tentative, even imprecise, explanations in science, so also will there be secure, well-established explanations. Thus, when we distinguish between theory and application in science, we are contrasting two essential concerns of science: concern with understanding nature, and concern with exploiting that theoretical understanding as a means of solving more practical, technological problems.

It is primarily at the level where new ideas about nature are proposed and tested that science and scientific method neatly fit our description. Yet there is an important, if by now obvious, connection between the worlds of theoretical and applied science. With very few exceptions, technical innovation springs from theoretical understanding. The scientists who designed, built, and tested the first nuclear reactors, for example, depended heavily on a great deal of prior theoretical and experimental work on the structure of the atom and the ways in which atoms of various sorts interact. Similarly, as one of our examples should serve to remind us, simple but effective new procedures for preventing the spread of disease were possible only after the theoretical work of Semmelweis and others began to yield some basic insight into the nature of germs and the ways in which diseases are spread.

Things to Come

In the chapters that follow, our central concern will be to expand this brief introductory account of scientific method. You will learn a good deal about both how to design and how to assess the results of good scientific tests. Along the way, we will look into what is involved in testing not only explanations but a number of other kinds of claims as well—notably, claims about causes and their effects and claims of extraordinary abilities. Does secondhand smoke cause lung cancer? Are psychics actually able to bend metal objects by sheer mind power or to discern the thoughts of others? These and many other interesting examples will be discussed as we fill in the details of our initial sketch of scientific method.

On our agenda will be a number of controversial topics, perhaps none more so than the distinction between legitimate and fraudulent applications of scientific method. Nothing can do more to lend an air of credibility to a claim than the suggestion that it has been "proven in scientific studies" or that it is "backed by scientific evidence." A sad fact, however, is that many claims made in the name of science are founded on gross misapplications of some aspect of scientific method. Indeed, so numerous are the ways in which scientific method can be abused that we will find it necessary to devote an entire chapter to fallacies commonly committed in attempting to marshal scientific evidence for questionable claims.

Our goals, then, in the chapters that follow are twofold. Our first and most important goal is to become familiar with the basic methodology common to all good scientific research. Our second goal is to learn to distinguish between legitimate and bogus applications of scientific method. Having accomplished these goals, you will find yourself more able to think clearly and critically about the claims of scientists and charlatans alike to have advanced our understanding of ourselves and our world.

Exercises

Try your hand at telling explanatory stories. The following exercises all describe curious things. See if you can come up with one or two explanations for each. Your explanation need not be true, but it must be such that, if it were true, it would explain the phenomenon in question.

1. A recent survey revealed that whereas 10% of all 20- year-olds are left-handed, only about 2% of all 75-year-olds are left-handed.

2. Have you ever noticed that baseball players tend to be superstitious? Batters and pitchers alike often run through a series of quite bizarre gestures before every pitch.

3. One of life's little sources of aggravation is the coiled phone cord. No matter how careful we are, it seems phone cords end up horribly twisted.[1]

4. In newspapers, magazines, and books, certain U.S. presidents are referred to by their initials whereas others are not. Why do newspapers refer to FDR and JFK and LBJ, but not RMN or JEC or RWR or GHWB?

5. Every once in a while, I come into possession of a quarter that has been painted red. Quarters are the only denomination of coin that are painted, and what is more, they are always painted red. Why would anyone do this?

Note

1. Exercises 3–5 are suggested by puzzles discussed in *Why Things Are: Answers to Every Essential Question in Life*, by Joel Achenbach (New York: Ballantine Books, 1991).

2

Testing Explanations

Explanations

Before we look into the process by which explanations are tested in science, we must do a bit of groundwork. We need to clear away some potential misunderstandings about the notion of an explanation. Along the way we shall also have something to say about what explanations do and do not involve and about what we can reasonably expect a scientific explanation to provide.

"Explanation" has several distinct senses. When we ask for an explanation, we could be asking for a number of things. If I'm late for an appointment with you, for example, you might ask me to *explain* why I'm late. Here, what you want is my justification—you want to know whether I have an excuse for being late. Or, to take another example, you might ask your math teacher to *explain* how to solve a particularly nasty problem. Here you are asking to be shown how to do something. But suppose, now, I were to bring to your attention the following rather curious fact: In many states, the letter *O* does not occur on automobile license plates. Your initial reaction might be to wonder why this is so, and you might well ask me to *explain*. Now you are asking not for the justification of something, nor to be shown how to do something, but for an account of why something is the case. In what follows, when we speak of an explanation, we are speaking neither of an excuse nor of how to do something. Rather, for our purposes, an explanation is an account of why something happened or continues to happen as it does.

An explanation is not the same thing as a hypothesis. Explanations in science are sometimes referred to as *explanatory hypotheses*, or simply *hypoth-*

eses, but many kinds of claims other than explanations are also called hypotheses. In the jargon of the scientist, just about any claim that may require testing before it is accepted will be called a hypothesis. Thus, if I believe there is intelligent life somewhere in the universe other than on earth, my belief constitutes a hypothesis of sorts, and there is nothing wrong with calling it that. It is not, however, an explanatory hypothesis. An explanatory hypothesis is a proposed explanation that needs to be tested.

New scientific explanations do not arise in an intellectual vacuum; they are occasioned by a desire to make sense of something that puzzles us. This point may seem so obvious as to hardly bear remarking. Plainly, if we understand something, there is no sense in attempting to provide a novel explanation for it. Yet two closely related points about the things that puzzle us are worth keeping in mind.

First, we must resist the temptation to think of the puzzling as that which is somehow strange and unfamiliar. Now, puzzling phenomena can indeed be strange and unfamiliar, even spectacularly so. In the late 1980s, for example, hundreds of circular and semicircular indentations were discovered in the wheat and corn fields of southern England. These large, regular patterns were called "crop circles," and there seemed to be no obvious explanation for their origin. There was no evidence, for example, that people made the circles; many occurred in the middle of crop fields where there were no obvious signs of human intrusion.[1] However, much that needs explaining is considerably less mysterious and unfamiliar. The world about us is filled with phenomena with which we are more than passingly familiar, but which we do not know how to explain.

We are all painfully familiar, for example, with many facts about AIDS—about how it is transmitted and what its effects are. Yet a great deal remains to be discovered about the nature of the virus and the way in which it attacks the human immune system. Perhaps nothing is more familiar in our lives than the simple fact that we are creatures capable of thought and feeling. Yet nothing is more puzzling than the way in which neurobiological processes in the human brain result in mental states such as those involved in thought and feeling. What these examples suggest is that both the unusual and the commonplace are ripe for scientific investigation. It has often been remarked that one of the talents of a good scientific researcher is the ability to discern those mundane bits and pieces of our daily lives whose investigation may yield new and important insight into the ways in which our world works.

Second, the fact that you or I am puzzled by something does not mean that it is genuinely puzzling. Once again, it may seem we are remarking the obvious. Yet, as we shall discover when we consider the way in which explanations are tested, it is not uncommon for a person to propose a novel explanation of something because he or she is unaware that somebody has already adequately explained the phenomenon in question.

Rarely, in science, does the need for explanation come to an end. An explanation tells us something about how or why a thing happens, but rarely will an explanation be so complete as to leave no further unanswered "whys" or "hows" about the thing in question. To see this, consider one basic sort of scientific explanation: explanation by reference to causal factors. We all know, for example, that the tides are caused, in part, by the gravitational attraction of the moon. Thus, we can explain the tides by reference to the facts that there is a large amount of water on the surface of the earth, that the earth rotates on its axis, and that the source of gravitational attraction (the moon) moves in orbit around the earth. Although our explanation clearly gives us a sense of why there should be two high and low tides roughly every 24 hours, it leaves a lot unexplained. What is the process by which gravitating bodies—in this case the moon and the oceans—interact? Put another way, how is it that massive objects such as these have an effect on one another? We might cite here something called the law of gravity: Objects tend to attract one another in direct proportion to their masses and in inverse proportion to the square of the distance between them. This mathematical relationship adds a bit of detail to our explanation. But why should this "law" hold? Why should objects attract one another at all, let alone in just this regular, lawlike fashion? Unfortunately, we must leave these questions unanswered, for little is yet known about what physicists today call the "carrier" of gravitational interaction, the graviton.

As this example suggests, explaining one thing in science often leads naturally to the need for new, more fundamental explanations. The moral of this is that in science, at any rate, progress is largely a matter of providing better and better approximations of what is going on in nature. Rarely are explanations final or complete in the sense of leaving no additional unanswered questions about what is really going on.

Scientific progress is not always a matter of supplementing received explanations with more subtle but complementary new explanations. The history of science is fraught with instances in which received explanations have been supplanted by novel and radically different ones. One of the most well-known examples of the replacement of one explanation with another is the gradual shift from the Ptolemaic conception of the universe to the Copernican.

According to the Ptolemaic view, systematized about A.D. 140 by Ptolemy Claudius of Alexandria, the stationary earth stands at the center of the universe and all heavenly objects revolve around the earth. The Ptolemaic view had considerable explanatory power in that, by a series of complicated calculations, the motions of all celestial objects known at the time—the sun, the moon, the five innermost planets, and the stars—could be explained, though in ways very different from the way we would explain them today. For example, careful observation revealed that Mars generally moves eastward across the night sky but occasionally appears to move backward for a bit before resuming its eastward course. According to the Ptolemaic view, all celestial objects trace out circular orbits around the earth. Ptolemy explained the backward, or retrograde, motion of Mars by introducing the notion of an epicycle—a small circular loop in the orbit of Mars such that, from an earthly perspective, Mars would actually appear to stop and then move backward during its epicycle. A tribute to its explanatory value is the fact that the Ptolemaic view dominated Western thought for more than a thousand years.

In the 16th century, however, Nicholas Copernicus, a Polish scientist and astronomer, proposed a new and radically different view of the cosmos. According to Copernicus, many of the basic assumptions of Ptolemy were wrong. The sun, not the earth, is at the center of things; two of the planets, Mercury and Venus, occupy orbits nearer the sun than does the earth; and, what is more, many celestial motions are to be explained by the fact that the earth rotates on its axis. One advantage of the Copernican view is that it suggests a very different explanation for retrograde motion than does the Ptolemaic. If, as Copernicus suggested, the orbit of Mars is outside that of the earth, then the double motion of Mars with respect to the earth explains the apparent backward motion of Mars. According to Copernicus, we observe the motion of Mars from a location that is itself moving through space, with the net effect that Mars will on occasion appear to be moving backward.

There are a number of interesting facts about this particular episode in the history of science. First is the fundamental change from Ptolemy to Copernicus in the way in which celestial motions were explained. But, though Copernicus was able to provide a remarkably accurate method of calculating the apparent motions of the planets, his great contribution came from the simplicity of his explanation compared to that of Ptolemy. By removing the earth from the center of the universe and replacing it with the sun, Copernicus was able to explain the motions of the stars and planets both with greater accuracy and in terms that required fewer peculiarities like the Ptolemaic epicycle.

But our story does not end here. Although, in rough outline, the Copernican view of the universe finally replaced that of Ptolemy, many of the details of the Copernican view were themselves eventually rejected. Like Ptolemy, for example, Copernicus believed that the planets trace circular orbits around the sun. (In fact, Copernicus, too, had to make use of the occasional epicycle to get his calculations of planetary motion to fit the best observations of the day.) It remained for Johann Kepler, nearly a century later, to discover that the planets trace elliptical orbits around the sun, thereby reducing the kinds of motion required to explain the observed positions of the planets and doing away, finally, with the infamous epicycle. In defense of Copernicus, it must be noted that Kepler had available much more accurate measurements of the movement of the planets than anything available to either Copernicus or Ptolemy. Yet, despite the enormous import of Kepler's contributions to our understanding of celestial motion, it remained for astronomers long after his time to refine the Copernican world view even further by removing the sun from its exalted position at the center of the universe.

Explanations in science can involve any of a number of distinct sorts of claims.   As we have said, an explanation tells us something about how or why an event or series of events happens or happened. To explain something is often to try to get at its cause or causes. Why, when we were small children, did teeth, carefully tucked under our pillows, vanish only to be replaced by money? Because while we were sleeping, our parents put the money there. Why is there a circular crater several miles in diameter in the Arizona desert? Because a large meteor survived intact its trip though the earth's atmosphere. So prevalent and basic is this method of explaining that it may seem that explanations, both in and out of science, must always involve statements about cause–effect relationships. In this view, to explain some event, E, is to cite prior events, $C_1, C_2, \ldots, C_n$, such that it is correct to say that E happened as a result of $C_1, C_2, \ldots, C_n$. $C_1, C_2, \ldots, C_n$ are, in this view, the causes of E and, thus, contain the explanation of E. Though it is no doubt tempting to think along these lines and to equate the process of explaining with that of getting at causes, this is a temptation we must resist. Explanations can and often do involve claims about effects and their causes, but they often involve a number of other kinds of claims. We can explain by reference to such things as *causal mechanisms, laws,* and *underlying processes.* Since each of these ways of explaining plays an important role in scientific inquiry, we must say a bit about how each is distinctive and how each is related to the others.

1. Causal mechanisms. We can know that one thing is the cause of another without fully understanding what is involved in the causal relationship. There is, for example, strong evidence for a causal link between cigarette smoking and lung cancer. This does not mean that cigarettes are the only causal factor nor that all cigarette smokers will contract the disease. Nevertheless, there can be little doubt that cigarettes are one of the major causes of lung cancer. Yet little is known about the *mechanism* —the physiological process—by which the carcinogens in cigarette smoke lead to uncontrolled cell growth in the lungs of the smoker. In science, explanations often involve claims about *causal mechanisms*—the processes intervening between cause and effect.

A recent study revealed an apparent causal connection between aspirin consumption and the risk of heart attack. According to the study, men who take a single buffered aspirin every other day have a 50% lower chance of having a heart attack than do men who do not take aspirin. Here the connection between aspirin consumption and risk of heart attack seems to be fairly well documented. As it turns out, the causal mechanism by which aspirin reduces the risk of heart attack is also well understood. Aspirin interferes with the first stage of the blood's clotting process. Now, many heart attacks are caused by blood clots in damaged arteries. It seems that when the thin inner wall of an artery is damaged, aspirin inhibits the tendency of minute blood platelets to clot over the damaged area. Thus, aspirin reduces the clotting effect that can lead to serious heart attack.

To take a very different example, one more closely related to the use of explanation by causal mechanism in our daily lives, imagine the following.[2] A friend applied for a job she really wanted. Yet now she tells us the job seems utterly uninteresting and she probably wouldn't accept it even if it were offered to her. Why the change in attitude? We discover subsequently that our friend learned she had no chance of getting the job. But how, if at all, did this bring about her change in attitude toward the job? The answer may well lie in a causal mechanism, often called cognitive dissonance reduction, that makes people cease desiring what they cannot get; you may be familiar with this mechanism under its more common name, "sour grapes." Having learned she wouldn't get the job, our friend adjusted her desires to reduce the dissonance caused by wanting something she could not have. No doubt the notion of cognitive dissonance reduction is a bit less precise than the mechanism invoked to explain the connection between aspirin and heart disease, and for that reason it would be more difficult to test. But such psychological mechanisms play an important role, nonetheless, in our attempts at explaining why people behave the way they do.

2. Laws. What happens if heat is applied to a closed container of a gas? Pressure increases. Why? An important law governing the behavior of gases, discovered by Joseph Gay-Lussac, provides the answer: If volume is held constant, the pressure exerted by a gas will vary directly with the temperature. So, as we increase the temperature of our gas by applying heat, we increase the pressure in the closed container. Such laws explain by revealing how particular events are instances of more general regularities in nature.

A law is *universal* when it claims that a particular kind of behavior will occur in all (or in no) cases. Thus, Gay-Lussac's law is universal in that it makes a claim about the behavior of all gases. But scientific laws need not be universal; some laws claim only that a particular kind of behavior will occur in a certain proportion of cases.

Suppose we were to learn that a good friend, a nurse, has contracted hepatitis B. We are aware that he works in a clinical setting where patients with hepatitis B are regularly treated. We are also aware that recent studies have shown that an alarmingly high number of health-care workers contract the hepatitis virus from their clients: One out of four health-care workers who are accidentally exposed to the virus will actually contract the disease.[3] It seems a real possibility that our friend's condition is explained, in part, by the statistic we have just cited. The explanation we might give would go something like the following:

> Exposed health-care workers have a 25% chance of contracting hepatitis B. Friend, F, is a nurse who works in a setting where the risk of exposure to hepatitis B is high. F has hepatitis B. Thus, it is likely that F has contracted hepatitis B from a client.

Here we have an example of explanation by law but where the law on which we rely is not universal. Remember, a universal law tells us that a particular kind of behavior will occur in all cases. Yet our law says that only 25% of exposed health-care workers, not all health-care workers, will contract the virus.

No doubt it seems odd to call this claim a "law," yet it is certainly lawlike, in the same way that Gay-Lussac's law is lawlike: Both describe a regular correspondence. In the case of Gay-Lussac's law, the correspondence is among the pressure, volume, and temperature of a gas; in the case of our hepatitis law, the correspondence is between workers who are exposed to the virus and workers who subsequently contract the disease. The difference is that laws of the latter sort, often called *statistical laws*, enable us to give explanations that must be carefully qualified. It may be that our friend has contracted the hepatitis virus from someone or something other than a client, and, as our statistical law tells us, chances are quite good that exposure to clients with the virus will not lead to infection. Thus, we had to qualify our explanation by adding the phrase "it is likely," to acknowledge the possibility that our explanation may be wrong in this particular case.

3. Underlying processes. You are probably aware that fluorescent lamps are much more efficient than traditional incandescent bulbs. The explanation lies in the way each produces light. When light is produced by an incandescent bulb, the following process takes place: Electrical energy passes through a wire, heating it until it incandesces (glows). The wire, called a filament, typically is made of a metal called tungsten; the enclosing bulb around the filament directs or diffuses the light. The problem is that 90% of the energy put into such a bulb is released in the form of heat, while only 10% results in light. Fluorescent lamps produce light in a different way, by energizing gas. Electrical energy flows into electrodes at the ends of a tube. The electrodes emit electrons, which energize a small amount of mercury vapor held at very low temperatures inside the tube. The energized mercury molecules radiate ultraviolet light, which is in turn absorbed by a phosphorescent coating on the inside of the surface of the tube, thus producing visible light. This process produces very little heat; fluorescent lamps are able to convert almost 90% of the energy they consume into light. So, the amount of electrical energy required by a fluorescent lamp to produce a given amount of light is substantially less than that required by an incandescent bulb.

The explanation we have just given has accounted for an observable phenomenon—the greater efficiency of fluorescent lights—by making reference to the process underlying the phenomenon being explained. Our explanation has involved electrons, electrodes, filaments, and gases and the way in which electrons behave under various conditions. In effect, we have explained one process by reference to what is occurring at a more fundamental level of the same process.

Explanation by reference to underlying processes is quite common in science, and something very much like it occurs in daily life as well. Suppose, for example, you discover a leaky faucet in your kitchen. You turn the faucet handle to the "off" position, but water continues to drip. So, having first turned off the water supply to the sink, you proceed to take the faucet apart and discover that one of the washers inside the shutoff valve is worn out. The explanation for the leaky faucet—the worn-out washer—involves a process that, in a sense, underlies the observed phenomenon.

Earlier we noted that in science the need for explanation rarely comes to an end. This fact is reflected in the interdependence of the types of explanation we have just considered. If, for example, we want to understand more about a particular causal connection, we will need to speculate about causal mechanisms that may be involved. A lake is polluted, and some of its indigenous species of wildlife begin to diminish. There seems to be a connection. But what is the process by which greater pollution leads to less and less wildlife?

Similarly, if we want to understand more about why a lawlike regularity obtains, we may need to consider underlying processes. Recall our discussion earlier of Gay-Lussac's law: If volume is held constant, the pressure exerted by a gas will vary directly with the temperature. Why, we might wonder, should this particular relationship among temperature, volume, and pressure hold for gases? The answer to this question requires that we examine the processes underlying the phenomenon described by our gas law. In fact, gases are composed of molecules rushing hither and thither at enormous speeds. Pressure on the container holding the gas is a result of gas molecules colliding with the walls of the container. When heat is applied to the container, it is translated into increased activity on the part of the gas molecules. The result is that the number of collisions with the container increases, thereby increasing the pressure exerted on the container by the gas. (This is a very rough sketch of a basic notion in what is called the kinetic theory of gases.)

Or if we want to understand more about a process underlying something, we may need to look once again for causal mechanisms and lawlike regularities considerably more fine-grained in character. To return for a moment to the process involved in fluorescent lighting, why do mercury molecules bombarded by electrons radiate ultraviolet light? To answer this question, we would need to consider the processes that intervene and perhaps even underlie the interaction of free electrons and mercury molecules.

You may well wonder whether the process of explanation can ever come to an end and, if so, where this end might be. These are deep and profoundly difficult philosophical issues. Some philosophers speculate that as a given science matures, claims about causal connections and mechanisms will be replaced gradually by broader and broader laws describing more and more causal phenomena. In this view, the most fundamental kind of scientific understanding is that provided when laws are discovered that reveal something about the interconnectedness of a wide variety of phenomena; the wider the variety, the greater the understanding. Other philosophers would maintain that, at least in certain sorts of cases, if not in all, to explain a thing is to identify its immediate cause or causes and that when we can find no further intervening mechanism, the process of explanation must come to an end. In this view, lawlike statements, no matter how broad and unifying, merely help us to classify and describe the more basic causal processes at work in nature. For our purposes, however, we need not wrestle with these deep philosophical issues. Suffice it to say, the kind of explanation one will give—whether it be about causes, causal mechanisms, laws, underlying processes, or something else—will depend on how much one knows and, of course, on what it is one wants to explain.

Many explanations do not need to be tested.   Consider, again, a puzzle discussed earlier—the rather curious fact that, in many states, the letter *O* is not used on license plates. Let me propose an explanation (E):

> Most states use numbers as well as letters on their license plates and the letter *O* could easily be confused with the numeral 0. Thus, the letter *O* is not used to avoid possible ambiguities in recording and reporting license-plate numbers.

E seems to clear up the puzzle—that is, if E is true. And there seems to be no obvious reason to think that E is not true. Certainly, E squares with what we know about the kind of concern that might prompt a large bureaucracy to adopt this sort of policy: the need to assign unique, unambiguous identification codes to large numbers of vehicles or people. No doubt we could verify E by making a few phone calls to the appropriate government agencies, but there would be little point in doing so, absent any reason to suppose E false.

By contrast, we would want to find some independent means of verifying an explanation when there is some substantial question as to its correctness. Now, we may question an explanation because we have some reason to believe it false. But more often our interest in a novel explanation is prompted by the simple fact that, though it "fits the facts"—though it would, if true, account for the phenomenon at issue—we just have no other reason to believe it true. The point of putting such an explanation to the test is, for the most part, to provide evidence in its favor beyond the fact of its potential to explain.

Preliminary Requirements

Prior to testing a novel explanation, we must satisfy ourselves that two crucial requirements have been met. First, there should be no question of the accuracy of the description of the phenomenon to be explained. Second, there should be no noncontroversial explanation available that allows us to account for the puzzling phenomenon. A noncontroversial explanation would be one, as in the license-plate case, that both clears up the puzzle and is itself highly plausible—an explanation we have independent reason to suppose true or, at any rate, no reason to doubt. So crucial are these two preliminary requirements that we need to consider each in more detail before turning to the question of what is involved in testing novel explanations.

Do we have an accurate description of the phenomenon to be explained?   Many people claim that strange things happen when the moon is full. One interesting and curious claim is that more babies are born on days when the moon is full or nearly full than at any other time of the month. Why do you suppose this is so? Is there something to astrology after all? Do the moon and the planets have an effect on our lives? Is it the gravitational pull of the moon tugging at the embryonic fluid surrounding the unborn child? Before beginning to speculate in this fashion about possible explanations, we would do well to back up a step. If it is true that more births occur near a full moon than at other times, we have a genuine mystery. But is it true? In fact, careful studies done at a number of hospitals strongly suggest that it is not. When birth rates were examined over a period of a year or two, it turned out that, on average, there were no more (and no fewer) births during the period near a full moon than during any other period. In a given month, there may be a few more (or less) births near a full moon than during other parts of the month, but when averaged out over a long period of time, the difference disappears—and with it, the need for any kind of explanatory speculation.

As it turns out, what is most interesting about this case has little to do with the puzzling phenomenon we were led to consider. What is more interesting is the question of why people might believe that there are more births during a full moon despite the clear evidence to the contrary. The answer lies in a common mistake people make in marshaling support for generalizations they believe to be true. This mistake is called *confirmation bias*. In supporting a general claim, such as "more births occur when the moon is full than at other times," it is easy to focus inadvertently on data that support the claim while ignoring data that suggest it may be false. Suppose, for example, that you and I work in a hospital maternity ward. We have both heard the claim in question, and we are aware that a number of our colleagues believe it. Under these conditions, it would be all too easy for us to think back and recollect only those experiences that tend to confirm the general proposition that more births occur when the moon is full.

Indeed, it would be difficult not to do this, for our tendency is to recall those experiences that are unusual or singular in their significance. I doubt, for example, that you can recall what you were doing on, say, February 8 last year, but I am confident you can recall something of what you did on the day you graduated from high school.

The selectivity with which we remember, coupled with the fact that we tend to look for evidence that confirms things we may already believe to be so, suggests that we should approach most generalizations with a certain amount of caution. We should be particularly skeptical of generalizations about the unusual and puzzling, like the claim about the moon and birth rates. Our initial impulse, in such cases, should be to consider the nature of the evidence for the claim. Close inspection of the evidence may reveal that something that initially appears to be puzzling is, after all, not so.

Most of us have had the disconcerting experience of receiving a phone call or visit from someone just as we were thinking of that person. Is some sort of mental telepathy involved here? Such experiences seem unusual and mysterious only if we fail to put them in perspective by considering the enormous number of times we have thought of someone and *not* received a phone call or visit from that person soon after. Given the number of times some person or other enters our thoughts, it seems entirely unremarkable that on occasion we will be contacted by a person we have been thinking about recently. If we think such events are evidence that something puzzling and not understood is going on, we are probably guilty of confirmation bias, concentrating on just those few events that seem to confirm the possibility of mental telepathy.

This is not to say that puzzling phenomena cannot be securely established. Suppose, for example, that the studies mentioned earlier about birth rates and the full moon had uncovered evidence that there are significantly more births when the moon is full than at other times. Then we would have a genuine mystery on our hands. The point here is that before accepting such a conclusion, we should insist on the sort of evidence provided by careful long-term observation that can correct for confirmation bias and the natural selectivity with which we remember.

Are more plausible rival explanations available?   Imagine that you are unable to find your keys. You have searched all morning to no avail, and you know they should be around the house somewhere because you remember using them to open the door when you came home late last night. One possible explanation is that you simply put them somewhere that you haven't looked yet. But other explanations are available as well. Perhaps someone who shares the house with you has inadvertently taken your keys instead of his or hers. These two explanations rival one another in that both, if true, would serve to explain the phenomenon in question. Presumably at least one of the two is wrong, though in just the right circumstances perhaps they might both be correct.

What makes one explanation more plausible than its rivals is a bit more difficult to say. Let's begin by considering a couple of explanations that are somewhat more bizarre than the two we have considered so far. Perhaps someone broke into your house while you were asleep and stole your keys. Or perhaps they just disappeared into thin air. Stranger things have been known to happen! Compare these two new explanations with the first explanation we proposed—that you have simply misplaced your keys. Our first explanation is at least fairly plausible, in that it makes no reference to other things that themselves stand in need of explanation. Surely you've misplaced things before, only to have them turn up after you were convinced they were lost forever.

Consider, next, the first of our more bizarre explanations: Somebody stole your keys. Keep in mind that the point of an explanation is to make sense of how or why something has happened. If in giving an explanation we invoke things that are themselves puzzling, we have only avoided the question of why the thing in question happened. Why would someone break into your house and take only your keys? And why is there no evidence of forced entry? Though these things could perhaps be explained—maybe we are dealing with an incredibly clever and skilled burglar who intends to return when you're not home—I think you can see that each additional explanation makes the original explanation seem less and less likely. Now, a whole string of events would have to occur in order for our second explanation to remain plausible. Our final explanation does no good at all. The keys have just "disappeared into thin air"? How does this work? Were they consumed by a tiny black hole? Did they spontaneously melt? A simple puzzle has now involved us in great mysteries.

In the jargon of the scientist, our two bizarre explanations violate a principle known as *Occam's razor*, named after a medieval philosopher and monk, William of Occam. Occam's razor says that given competing explanations—any of which would, if true, explain a given puzzle—we should initially opt for the explanation that itself contains the least number of puzzling notions. By comparison with our two bizarre explanations, our first explanation—that you put your keys somewhere you haven't looked yet—fits the bill here. So, to say that one of a series of rival explanations is the most plausible is to say it is the one most in keeping with Occam's razor. Keep in mind that Occam's razor does not rule out explanations that involve notions not fully understood; it only suggests that, given competing explanations, we should favor the one that involves the least number of problematic notions. If one were forced to choose between clever burglars and black holes to account for the missing keys, Occam's razor would suggest the former choice.

Interestingly enough, we could, under the right circumstances, appeal to Occam's razor to help us think about our first two explanations for the missing keys. Suppose, for example, that your roommate rarely, if ever, takes things belonging to you, inadvertently or otherwise. Suppose, too, that you are constantly misplacing things. Under these circumstances, Occam's razor would suggest that, all things considered, we should favor the first of our explanations. In the circumstances we have imagined, that is, it seems more likely that you, not your roommate, are to blame for the missing keys.

Searching for more plausible rival explanations before going on to test a novel explanation may bear some unexpected fruit. Several years ago, a resident of Seattle, Washington, commented in a letter to the editor of the city's major daily newspaper that something was causing tiny scratches and pockmarks in the windshield of his car. Subsequent letters from other readers confirmed that this phenomenon was widespread. Further letters and articles attempted to explain this puzzle. People speculated about everything from acid rain to industrial pollutants to mysterious new chemicals used to deice the roads in winter. In fact, the correct explanation was considerably simpler. The effect of the initial letter to the editor was to encourage people to look *at* their windshields instead of *through* them. People were actually looking at their windshields closely for the first time and noticing marks and scratches that had accumulated over the years.

An additional advantage to the search for plausible rival explanations becomes apparent when we consider what happens if our quick check for rival explanations turns up nothing. In the fact that we cannot "explain away" the phenomenon in question, we have some initial evidence that we are on the right track with our proposed explanation. This brings us to the central topic of this chapter.

How to Test an Explanation

In Chapter 1, we spoke of explanatory stories rather than of explanations. Our point was to emphasize the tentativeness with which novel explanations are issued. Suppose, then, that we have a novel explanation, call it E, for some puzzling state of affairs. We are confident that we have accurately described the puzzling phenomenon, and we know of no plausible rival explanation. How do we determine whether E is the correct explanation for our puzzle?

To test E, we need to design an experiment that will provide some sort of independent evidence either for or against E. The fact that E, if correct, would explain our puzzle is not evidence that E is correct. The puzzling facts that E attempts to account for may be consistent with a number of other explanations and, thus, cannot be construed to provide evidence for or against any one of them. What we need to come up with is a set of experimental conditions under which we can predict that something very specific will occur if E is the correct explanation but will not if E is incorrect. Recall for a moment our earlier discussion of the puzzle involving your missing keys. One explanation we proposed was that your roommate had inadvertently taken your keys. The fact that your keys are missing is not evidence that this explanation is correct. Remember the other explanations we considered. Since all of our proposed explanations stand in the same relation to the puzzling facts, the puzzling facts cannot be construed to provide evidence for the correctness of any of the explanations.

What would provide evidence would be something like the following: We begin by *assuming* your roommate has taken your keys. Based on this assumption, if we could contact your roommate and ask about the keys, we could make a very specific prediction: Your roommate would acknowledge having taken your keys by mistake. Were your roommate to acknowledge this, we would have independent evidence for the explanation at issue. Conversely, if your roommate were to deny having taken the keys, we would have evidence that the explanation must be mistaken.

This is roughly the strategy followed in designing tests for explanations in science. First, we attempt to arrive at a set of experimental conditions under which we can predict that something quite specific (1) will happen if the explanation is correct and (2) will not happen if the explanation is wrong. In other words, we want to try to arrive at a set of experimental conditions under which the predicted result will occur *if and only if* the explanation at issue is correct.

Our prediction, of course, must be something other than the puzzling facts we are trying to explain. Ideally, a good test of an explanation should satisfy the requirements implicit in both (1) and (2). If both (1) and (2) are satisfied in the design of an experiment, the results of the experiment will reveal either that the explanation at issue is correct or that it is mistaken. To see this, consider the conclusion we are entitled to draw if an experiment meets our two requirements. First, imagine that we fail to get the predicted result: (1) tells us that if the proposed explanation is right, we ought to get our result; since we did not get the result, we have evidence that our explanation must be wrong. Next, imagine that we do get the predicted result: (2) tells us that if the proposed explanation is wrong, we should expect to get something other than the predicted result; since we did get the predicted result, we can conclude that the explanation must be right.

Ideally, as we said, a good test of an explanation should satisfy both (1) and (2). Unfortunately, we do not live in an ideal world, and rarely, if ever, do actual experiments provide the kind of decisive evidence our experimental strategy promises. In the real world in which scientific experiments are actually carried out, it would be nearly impossible, for example, to arrive at a prediction that simply could not occur if the explanation at issue were wrong. In anything other than unrealistic and utterly ideal conditions, things can and do happen to upset our expectations. Even in the case of the missing keys, things could happen to undermine our test results. Perhaps your roommate is unwilling to admit taking your keys or is unaware of having done so. Either of these possibilities means that our proposed test may not provide totally conclusive evidence for or against our explanation.

Our experimental strategy is of value, then, not because it sets a realistic standard, but because it provides us with an idealized standard against which we can assess the design of actual experiments. The closer an actual experiment comes to meeting our two requirements, given the constraints of the real world, the better is its design.

A Case Study

Let us apply what we have said so far about the design of a good experiment to an actual case. One of the more interesting episodes in the history of science involves the theory of spontaneous generation. As recently as the late 1800s, many people believed that living organisms could be generated from nonliving material. One physician in the 17th century, for example, claimed that mice arose from a dirty shirt and a few grains of wheat placed in a dark corner. Similarly, it was thought that maggots—tiny, white, wormlike creatures, the larval stage of common houseflies—were generated spontaneously out of decaying food. In 1688, an Italian physician, Francisco Redi, published a work in which he challenged the doctrine that decaying meat will eventually turn into flies. The following passage is from Redi's *Experiments in the Generation of Insects*:

> I began to believe that all worms found in meat were derived directly from the droppings of flies, and not from the putrefaction of meat, and I was still more confirmed in this belief by having observed that, before the meat grew wormy, flies had hovered over it, of the same kind as those that later bred in it. Belief would be vain without the confirmation of experiment, hence in the middle of July I put a snake, some fish, some eels from the Arno and a slice of milk-fed veal in four large wide-mouthed flasks; having well closed and sealed them, I then filled the same number of flasks in the same way, only leaving these open. It was not long before the meat and fish, in these second vessels, became wormy and flies were seen entering and leaving at will; but in the closed flasks I did not see a worm though many days had passed since the dead flesh had been put in them.[4]

This passage gives us Redi's explanation for the maggots, a description of the experiment he carried out to test his explanation, and his test results.

To determine whether Redi's experiment meets our criteria for a good test, it will be useful to have at our disposal a concise description of the explanation, the experimental conditions, and the prediction involved in Redi's experiment. In the preceding passage, Redi provides us with his results, rather than his predicted results, but we can easily extrapolate back to the prediction Redi had in mind when designing his experiment.

Explanation: Worms are derived directly from the droppings of flies. (E_1)
Experimental conditions: Two sets of jars are filled with meat or fish. One set is sealed; the other is left open so that flies can enter the jars. (EC_1)
Prediction: Worms (maggots) will appear only in the second set of jars. (P_1)

Earlier we pointed out that a good test of an explanation is one in which, under the right experimental conditions, we can predict that something quite specific

(1) *will* happen if the explanation is correct, and
(2) will *not* happen if the explanation is wrong.

So, we must ask two questions about Redi's experiment.

(1') If E_1 is correct, is it highly likely that P_1 will occur under EC_1?
(2') If E_1 is wrong, is it highly *unlikely* that P_1 will occur under EC_1?

The answer to (1') is relatively easy. If the worms are derived from the droppings of flies, it would seem highly likely that only the meat in the open containers would develop worms. But assume for the moment that Redi's predicted results did not obtain. Assume that worms appeared in the sealed containers as well, or that no worms appeared in the exposed meat. It is at least possible that E_1 could be true even if P_1 failed to occur. It may be, for example, that the seals were not perfect, in which case fly droppings could have contaminated the sealed jars; or it may be that flies did not lay eggs in the open containers. Thus, a failed prediction can be taken to suggest that E_1 is incorrect only if certain *auxiliary assumptions* are made—namely, that neither of these two things has actually happened. Since precautions could be taken to ensure that the seals were perfect, and it seems highly unlikely that flies would somehow avoid the open containers of meat, the failure of P_1 to obtain would seem to provide quite decisive evidence against E_1.

Would a failure to achieve the predicted result have absolutely ruled out E_1? No. It is always possible that other things—things of which we are not aware—could occur to undermine this conclusion. But other possibilities seem remote, and, on balance, a failed prediction would seem to constitute reasonably strong evidence against E_1.

Now consider (2'). If E_1 is wrong, is it highly *unlikely* that P_1 will occur under EC_1? If worms are *not* derived from the droppings of flies, does it seem highly unlikely that worms would develop only in the open containers? At first blush, it may seem that the answer to (2') is straightforward. If the worms are produced by some process internal to the meat and fish, not by fly droppings, it would seem highly improbable that worms would develop only in those containers left exposed to the air. Thus, if the predicted result occurs, it seems we have strong evidence that E_1 must be correct. It would just be too much of a coincidence if the predicted results occurred even though E_1 is incorrect.

However, things are not always as straightforward as they seem. Many scientists of Redi's time believed in the doctrine of spontaneous generation and looked upon his results with some suspicion. They speculated that there might be some "active principle" in the air necessary for spontaneous generation. By depriving the meat and fish in the sealed containers of a sufficient flow of fresh air, they reasoned, Redi may have inadvertently prevented the spontaneous generation of worms. So, despite the fact that Redi's experimental results seem to confirm E_1, they might still be consistent with the doctrine of spontaneous generation.

In light of this line of speculation, the answer to (2') must be carefully qualified. If E_1 is wrong, it is highly unlikely that P_1 will occur under EC_1, but only if we make certain auxiliary assumptions. The major assumption, of course, is that there is no "active principle" in the air necessary for the spontaneous generation of worms in meat. But there is a larger and more nebulous assumption we must make here, to the effect that spontaneous generation does not involve any other process that Redi may have tampered with or overlooked in setting up his experiment. Thus, the occurrence of P_1 constitutes evidence for E_1 only if we can be reasonably sure that our auxiliary assumptions hold.

Our examination of the work of Francisco Redi, given our two requirements for optimal experimental design, suggests that Redi's results were not entirely decisive. Based on Redi's experiment, we can be certain neither of the truth of his explanation nor of the falsehood of the doctrine of spontaneous generation. This much, however, we can say: Redi designed and carried out an experiment that provided strong initial evidence of something amiss in the doctrine of spontaneous generation. Redi certainly made clear the kind of assumption that would have to hold if the doctrine of spontaneous generation were to remain viable. Something like an "active principle" in the air would need to be worked out and tested if the doctrine of spontaneous generation were to survive mounting experimental evidence that it was wrong. In fact, Redi found a simple and quite decisive way of testing for this active principle, but that is another story—one, by the way, that you will be asked to think about in just a bit. But our story has a happy ending. Building on the work of Redi and others, later researchers were able to dispatch the doctrine of spontaneous generation by using a new scientific instrument—the microscope—to make careful observations of bacteria and other microorganisms not visible to Redi.

Several points about the nature of scientific experimentation are nicely illustrated by the example we have just considered. First, the results of a single experiment rarely provide decisive confirmation of an explanation. Rather, they often produce a tentative finding and point in the direction of needed further experimentation, much as Redi's experiment pointed to the need for a further experiment involving free-flowing air.

Second, even if the results of an experiment are negative, we need not conclude that the explanation is wrong. We have at our disposal a number of alternatives. Imagine, for example, that we have carried out an experiment but have failed to get the result we predicted. We could conclude, of course, that our proposed explanation is wrong. But we need not conclude this, at least yet. Instead, we might consider one of two things: Either we have made an auxiliary assumption we are not entitled to make, or the experimental conditions were somehow compromised. In our example, failure to properly seal the first set of containers would constitute a defect in the experimental conditions; the assumption that freely circulating air is not required for spontaneous generation might constitute an auxiliary assumption that bears closer examination. By this maneuver, we may be able to "save" an explanation that appears, under experimental scrutiny, to be wrong. However, if there are no questionable auxiliary assumptions and no reason to believe the experiment flawed, such holding maneuvers will do little good. The point here is that, in designing an experiment, it is important to be aware both of potentially questionable auxiliary assumptions associated with the explanation and of possible weaknesses in the experimental design.

Finally, a good experiment need not be one that confirms the explanation at issue. Had Redi's experimental results been contrary to his prediction, and had all attempts to "save" the explanation failed, his experiment would nonetheless have been a good one. The point of an experiment is to provide decisive results, one way or the other, given the constraints of the real world. A good experiment, then, will tell us when an explanation is right, or at least on the right track, but it will also tell us when a proposed explanation is in all likelihood wrong.

On occasion, an experimental result will be at odds with a well-established explanation. Such a result, by itself, must be looked at with some skepticism. Not too long ago, for example, a team of scientists discovered that a gyroscope, spun in just the right way, appeared to lose weight—a result at odds with the law of gravity. (See Chapter 5, Exercise 29, for more on this case.) Yet even the experimenters registered some skepticism about their results. One way to check controversial experimental results is by *replication*—by having others attempt to reproduce the results in different experimental settings. If the same or similar results can be obtained by other experimenters, chances are good that there are no obvious flaws in the original experimental design nor in the techniques used to carry out the original experiment. By contrast, failure to reproduce the original results in a new experimental setting suggests, at the very least, that the original experiment may be flawed.

The gyroscope experiment was reported in a well-known scientific journal, *Physical Review Letters*. The results reported in such journals serve as a sort of recipe for the experiment. The experimenters provide a step-by-step account of the experiment, often including discussion of important auxiliary assumptions. Thus, scientific journal articles provide other experimenters with a detailed account of the experimental design, thereby providing both information necessary to assess the experiment and a recipe for reproducing the results.

How Not to Test an Explanation: A Case Study

If you have a pet cat or dog, you may have noticed that on occasion your pet seems to react to things before they happen and sometimes even seems to know what you are thinking. Whenever I'm angry, for example, my cat seems to sense it and makes a point of avoiding me. When I'm in a good mood, she invariably follows me around, hoping for attention and snacks. Is it possible that extrasensory perception (ESP) is the explanation for this remarkable behavior?

Consider the following test, proposed in a book entitled *Test Your ESP:*

> At mealtime you might put out two feedpans instead of one for your dog or cat. The feedpans should be located so that they are equally convenient to the animal. They should be placed six to eight inches apart. Both should contain the same amount of food and avoid using a feedpan the animal is familiar with. Pick the dish you wish the animal to eat from and concentrate on it. In this test, the animal has a 50% chance of choosing correctly half the time. You may want to keep a record of his responses over several weeks to determine how well your pet has done.[5]

The explanation at issue here is that animals are receptive to human thoughts via ESP, and the prediction is that under the experimental conditions described, a pet will pick the dish its owner is thinking of more than 50% of the time. (Not "a 50% chance . . . half the time," as the author of the passage claims!)

Assume now that cats and dogs do indeed have ESP. Does it follow that our experimental subject should pick the bowl we are thinking of more than 50% of the time? In other words, is it clear that we have isolated a result that ought to occur provided the explanation at issue is correct? Yes, but only if one highly questionable auxiliary assumption is granted. Suppose you were to say to your pet, in an entirely monotonous tone of voice, "Eat out of the red dish, the dish on the left, Fido." I doubt Fido would grasp the meaning of the words you have uttered. Domestic animals tend to react to a complex of behavioral cues, some given by vocal inflection, but not to the meaning of words uttered in their presence. Thus, if saying "Eat out of the red dish" out loud will not do the trick, it is doubtful that thinking the same thing silently will work. Nor will it do to "picture" the red bowl in your "mind's eye." I doubt Fido would react in the appropriate way to an actual picture of the red bowl, so it seems highly unlikely that Fido would react to a "mental picture" of it. Thus, our prediction seems to follow from our proposed explanation only if we make a questionable assumption—namely, that animals can understand human thoughts and words.

In addition, it does not seem all that unlikely that our subject might pick the correct bowl more than 50% of the time even if our proposed explanation is false. A number of things could happen, any of which would account for our subject's success. Here are only a few. First, suppose that our subject tends to go to one bowl instead of the other. It is possible that the experimenter, who is both sending the instructions and observing the outcome, will inadvertently think of the dish the pet favors. Second, domestic animals are very good at discerning nonverbal cues. It may be that the experimenter is inadvertently looking at or standing in the direction of the dish being thought about and that the experimental subject is picking up these cues. Finally, recall our discussion of confirmation bias earlier in this chapter. Something very much like confirmation bias may be at work here. Suppose that our experimenter was convinced in advance of doing the experiment that animals have ESP. In recording or evaluating the subject's responses, the experimenter may inadvertently leave out responses that would otherwise provide evidence against animal ESP.

As we said earlier, a good test of an explanation is one in which, under the right experimental conditions, we can predict that something quite specific (1) will happen if our explanation is correct and (2) will not happen if our explanation is wrong. The prediction associated with our ESP experiment satisfies the first condition only if we grant an entirely questionable auxiliary assumption. But the design of the experiment leaves open so many loopholes—so many ways for the predicted result to occur even if the explanation at issue is false—that the second of our two conditions is not met at all. A good test, like Redi's, will provide evidence one way or the other about the explanation at issue. A poorly designed test, like our pet-ESP test, will leave us precisely where we began—with little reason to think one way or the other about the explanation being tested.

Summary

We have covered a lot of material in this chapter. So before concluding, a brief review is in order. Here is a summary of what is involved in testing an explanation. Prior to undertaking any sort of test of a novel explanation, we must do a bit of preliminary work. First, we must determine that we have an accurate description of the phenomenon to be explained. Next, we hunt for more plausible rival explanations. If by either of these moves we cannot "explain away" the phenomenon, we are ready to design a test for our novel explanation.

Let's quickly review the key ideas involved in constructing a good experiment:

Experimental conditions: a description of the experiment we propose to carry out.

The prediction: what we expect to happen, under our experimental conditions, if the explanation at issue is correct.

Auxiliary assumptions: any assumptions we must make in conjunction with our experiment; assumptions that must hold if either a failed or a successful prediction is to provide decisive results about the proposed explanation.

In a well-designed experiment, the prediction will be

(1) highly probable if the explanation is correct, and
(2) highly improbable if the explanation is mistaken.

Whenever possible, we need to make explicit any questionable auxiliary assumptions required if the prediction is to follow from our explanation. Finally, it is always a good idea to reexamine our experimental design in light of any questionable assumptions; it may be possible to modify the experiment so that questionable assumptions are not required.

The exercises that follow all involve puzzling phenomena and proposed explanations for them. Your task is to design effective tests for these explanations. To complete the exercises, you will need to become adept at applying the ideas with which we have been working. But if you work carefully though the exercises, you will develop a clear grasp of the process involved in designing tests for explanations. In the next two chapters we will work with variations of the method we have developed as we begin to think about ways of testing claims other than explanations.

Exercises

The following exercises each contain a set of puzzling facts and a proposed explanation of those facts. Work carefully through each exercise, doing all of the following:

  a. *State the facts to be explained and the proposed explanation.*
  b. *Answer the following preliminary questions:*
   (1) *Are the facts of the case as they appear to be?*
   (2) *Can you think of any reason to believe that the facts misrepresent what is going on?*
   (3) *If so, how can we determine what the facts are?*
   (4) *Do any more plausible rival explanations come to mind? What are they?*
  c. *If you are satisfied that we have a real puzzle, design an experiment in which the explanation given in the exercise can be tested. In other words, imagine a set of experimental conditions and an accompanying prediction that is (1) highly probable provided the explanation is correct and (2) highly improbable provided the explanation is mistaken.*
  d. *Think carefully about any auxiliary assumptions that may be required by your experiment and that may themselves be questionable. Are there things you may be assuming to be true that, if false, would undermine your results?*
  e. *Modify the design of your experiment in light of any questionable assumptions you have unearthed.*
  f. *If you have identified a plausible rival explanation, design a test for that explanation that meets the conditions set forth in step c.*

(Note: On page 32 a solution is provided for Exercise 1. Look it over carefully to get a sense of how to solve the other problems.)

1. Recently I have noticed something peculiar and really quite irritating about my doctor. If my appointment is scheduled early in the day, I usually see my doctor within a few minutes of the appointed time. But when my appointment is scheduled later in the day,

I've spent as much as an extra hour sitting in the waiting room or waiting in the examination room. I think I know what the problem is. Whenever I come in for an appointment, my doctor insists on catching up on the details of my life; he asks about my work, my family, how much I'm exercising, even if I've seen any interesting movies or read any good books lately. It seems clear to me that my doctor spends too much time "chatting" with his patients about things not related to the problems they are there to see him about. As a result, he falls further and further behind as the day goes on.

2. As you know, Francisco Redi claimed that the worms found on rotting fish and meat are the result of eggs dropped by flies. As you also know, Redi's claim was not universally accepted. Redi's critics hypothesized that there might be something in freely circulating air, something we might call an "active principle," that must be present if spontaneous generation is to occur. (Hint: The explanation to be tested here is not Redi's but the one proposed by his critics.)

3. It is well known that college students who turn in typed assignments tend to get better grades than those students who turn in handwritten assignments. I suppose this is understandable. Good students—students who are bright and responsible and who take their studies seriously—are willing to go that extra step. Not only do they do superior work, they take great pains to ensure that it is submitted in the most attractive, readable format possible.

4. Few people would disagree, I think, that the quality of television programming in this country is dismal. What really irks me is that the few programs I want to watch are invariably all on at the same time. Weeks and weeks go by when all there is to watch is so much junk: mindless, homogeneous sitcoms, vacuous dramas, and newscasts that are nothing more than collections of headlines with little substance. And then, every once in a while, a whole series of quality programs—specials, good films, and so on—will be broadcast, virtually all at the same time. But I think I've finally figured it out. A large sample of TV viewers like you and me are polled two or three times a year to determine the number of people watching the various networks. These polls are taken during what are called "sweeps weeks." So all the networks hoard their best programs to show during a sweeps week, when they are all competing for the largest share of the audience. The result, of course, is that all the best programming is shown at the same time.

5. From time to time, one hears stories of strange, almost unbelievable animal behavior. Pets, for example, seem to sense when their master is about to return. Dogs and cats have been known to move their young to a safe place just before an earthquake. There are many documented cases in which animals have reacted strangely to their impending death or that of their masters. These incidents involve knowledge that came to the animals in some apparently paranormal way. There is no apparent explanation for them—except ESP.

6. Did you know that the U.S. Treasury still prints two-dollar bills? I know it's hard to believe because you rarely see them in circulation. The problem is that whenever a new batch of two-dollar bills is distributed, people are struck by their novelty and hoard them, thus taking the two-dollar bills out of circulation as soon as they appear.

7. When I opened the bread drawer this morning, I found to my dismay a tiny hole in the cellophane in which the bread was packaged. There were, in addition, a number of crumbs spread out in the area of the hole. No doubt about it, there must be a mouse loose somewhere in the kitchen.

8. A fact of life in large organizations, whether in the private or the public sector, is that an enormous number of people are doing jobs for which they are not qualified. This is because of what is often called the "Peter Principle." People tend to rise to the level of their incompetence. In a large organization, if you are good at what you do, you will be promoted. And if you are competent at your new job, you will be promoted once again. This process of advancement stops only when a person rises to a position in which he or she is not fully competent. Lacking competence, the person will do a poor job and thus not be promoted further. So a person's final position in a large organization will be a position that he or she is not qualified to fill.

9. In four of the past five presidential elections, Americans have elected the taller of the two major-party candidates. It is distressing that height is one of the more important qualifications for the presidency. But let's face it, we live in a society in which something as superficial as height can make a difference in our attitude toward a person. The taller you are, the better are your chances for success.

10. Many of you have probably played with a Ouija board. On a rectangular board approximately 2 feet by 3 feet are printed all of the letters of the alphabet, the numbers from 1 to 10, and the words *yes* and *no*. A small, plastic, three-legged stool, called the planchette, is placed on the Ouija board. Two people, sitting at opposite sides of the board, rest the tips of their fingers gently on opposite ends of the planchette. Somebody then asks the spirit of the Ouija board a question, and what follows is startling. The planchette slowly begins to move, often spelling out an answer to the question! What is more, the answer is frequently something that neither of the participants has any way of knowing. The spirit may even predict something that is yet to happen. As anybody who has played with the Ouija board will attest, one has the distinct feeling that the planchette is actually pulling the hands of the participants about the board; the participants do not feel as though they are pushing the planchette. Well, this is just wrong. In fact, the participants are moving the planchette. The eerie feeling of being dragged about the board results from the fact that each participant is exerting only half as much effort as it would take a single person to move the planchette. The resulting impression—that something else is doing the work is thus understandable. But this "something else" is not the spirit of the Ouija; it is the person on the other end of the planchette.

11. A recent telephone survey of 113,000 Americans about religious affiliation produced some rather interesting facts. Perhaps the most interesting was that whereas 7.5% of the respondents nationwide said they belonged to no church, 15% of those sampled in Oregon, Washington, and California claimed no religious affiliation. It seems clear that all the "new age" mumbo jumbo that goes on out West is turning people away from God.

12. Recently, a good friend quit her job. This is surprising because her income was in the six-figure range as a partner in a large law firm. And guess what she is doing now? She

sold her home and bought a tiny, primitive cabin in the woods, where she lives alone and claims to be studying to become a Buddhist monk! She says she has enough money put away to live for a year or so, and afterwards doesn't know what she is going to do. This amazes me because she has always been such a responsible person. You know what I think? She's undergoing a good old-fashioned midlife crisis.

13. The following is from a newspaper editorial entitled "Books Now Being Sold by the Pound":

> According to assurances by the publishers, Norman Mailer's new novel, *Harlot's Ghost,* is tough to put down. It is also, at 1,328 pages, no snap to pick up. And when you put it down, you might want to make sure there are no small children underneath.
>
> Mailer's new book is the most dramatic example of ink inflation, the new tendency for books to come in at a size and heft that used to be reserved for stereo speakers. Currently, a good middle-weight novel can run 800 pages.
>
> The strange thing about this epidemic of book bloat is that books are getting longer just as, everyone agrees, the time spent reading is getting shorter. At two minutes a page, *Harlot's Ghost* would fill up about 50 hours, which is just about the total annual reading time of entire American age groups.
>
> People have several ideas on why books are getting so much longer than the average attention span. Basically, of course, the reason is technology.
>
> Right now, most books are written on word processors, meaning that by pushing a single button the writer can turn a research note into a page. It also means that writing on at length is essentially painless, except for the person who tries to read it.
>
> Back when people wrote with quill pens, or even with manual typewriters, writers had to think a little more about whether what they were about to say was worth the effort of writing it. Not surprisingly, the calculation made for shorter books.[6]

14. The following story appeared about an advertisement in a weekly newsmagazine as well as in the local newspapers. It seems that the Pepsi-Cola Company decided that Coke's 3-to-1 lead in Dallas was no longer acceptable, so Pepsi commissioned a taste preference study. The participants, chosen from Coke drinkers in the Dallas area, were asked to express a preference for a glass of Coke or a glass of Pepsi. The glasses were not labeled "Coke" and "Pepsi" because of the obvious bias that might be associated with a cola's brand name. Rather, in an attempt to administer the two drinks in a blind fashion, the Coke glass was simply marked with a Q and the Pepsi glass with an M. Results indicated that more than half chose Pepsi over Coke. It seems clear that when the effects of advertising are set aside, cola drinkers prefer the taste of Pepsi to Coke.[7]

15. Arturo Toscanini died a few weeks short of his 90th birthday. Leopold Stokowski died at age 95. If you think of symphony conductors as a long-lived group, you are correct. According to a major life insurance company study of 319 conductors living in 1990, 21 were 80 years or older, and 3 were more than 90 years old. The study also found that the average life span of a conductor was several years longer than that of people in other

occupational groups. The insurance company concluded: "The exceptional longevity enjoyed by symphony conductors lends further support to the theory that work fulfillment and recognition of professional accomplishments are important determinants of health and longevity."

A Solution to Exercise 1

(Note: Don't simply accept this solution. Satisfy yourself that the experiment it describes is a good one!)

a. *State the facts to be explained and the proposed explanation.* The fact to be explained is my doctor's failure to stay on schedule. The explanation proposed is that he spends much of the allotted time with his patients discussing extraneous things.

b. **(1)** *Are the facts of the case as they appear to be?* This is hard to say, but one thing does seem clear. I believe that my doctor is routinely late. However, most people don't go to the doctor all that often and I am no exception. So it seems likely that my belief is based on only a small number of observations.

(2) *Can you think of any reason to believe that the facts misrepresent what is going on?* Apart from the possibility mentioned in b(1), it may be that I have simply remembered only those few aggravating instances in which I have been kept waiting and that they have occurred late in the day by coincidence.

(3) *If so, how can we determine what the facts are?* We could keep a record for a month or so of all appointments and the actual times that patients are seen.

(4) *Do any more plausible rival explanations come to mind? What are they?* Assuming that something like the investigation described in b(3) determines that my doctor does routinely fall further and further behind schedule, I can think of several rival explanations. (I'm sure you can think of others.) One is that emergencies often require that the doctor take time away from his scheduled patients. Another explanation (actually suggested by a doctor) is that clients frequently schedule appointments to deal with a single ailment but during the examination bring up other problems that require additional time to investigate.

c. *Design an experiment in which the explanation given in the exercise can be tested.* The explanation at issue is that my doctor spends too much time talking with his patients about things having no obvious bearing on the problem for which the patient is being seen. Keep in mind that we are not trying to establish whether or not my doctor "chats" too much with his patients. Rather, we are trying to determine whether extraneous "chatting" is the reason he falls behind schedule. We might test this explanation in the following way. First, we will need to obtain the doctor's cooperation. Suppose, then, we were to instruct him to consciously refrain from speaking with patients about things not directly related to the problems that brought them to his office. We might videotape (with patients' permission, of course) all the appointments for a week. If the explanation at issue is correct, we would predict that my doctor will, under these conditions, stay on schedule or at least come closer to staying on schedule.

In this experiment, the prediction seems both highly probable provided the explanation is correct and highly improbable if it is mistaken or wrong. If extraneous "chatting" with patients is the correct explanation, we would expect time per appointment to decrease. Moreover, if the explanation is wrong, it seems highly unlikely that we could reduce time per visit by simply limiting the amount of extraneous chatting.

d. *Think carefully about any auxiliary assumptions that may be required and that may themselves be questionable.* One important but rather nebulous auxiliary assumption comes to mind here. Our experiment involves the assumption that the instructions we have given the doctor—indeed, the doctor's knowledge that he is taking part in an experiment—will have no effect on the way in which he works. It seems possible that he will inadvertently work more quickly because he is nervous or aware of being part of the experiment. If that is the case, any improvement noted over the course of the experiment may be due to factors other than that for which we are testing.

e. *Modify the design of your experiment in light of any questionable auxiliary assumptions you have unearthed.* Asking the doctor to work at a normal pace may just make things worse. However, we might take the precaution of taping a week of appointments prior to giving the doctor his instructions. We can then use that week's tape as a rough benchmark against which to judge whether he is performing at a normal rate during the week of the experiment.

f. *If you have identified a plausible rival explanation, design a test for that explanation that meets the conditions set forth in step c.* If our test yielded negative results—that is, if under the conditions we have described my doctor continues to fall behind—we might want to consider one of the rival explanations proposed in b(4). The most likely is the suggestion that clients routinely want to discuss ailments in addition to those they have indicated when making their appointments.

The details of an effective test for this explanation are not too difficult to work out. Again, we should clarify what we are testing. At issue is not whether people complain of additional maladies but whether such complaining is the source of the problem we are investigating. To this end we might design an experiment that involves instructing the doctor to deal only with the problem for which a patient is seeing him. Or we might instruct the person who schedules appointments to make sure that patients give a complete inventory of problems prior to their visit. Of course, care must be taken to ensure that our prediction meets the conditions in step c.

Notes

1. In fact, there is now evidence that some of the crop circles are manmade. Several people claim to have made circles and have demonstrated to the British media how to make them.
2. This example is adapted from *Nuts and Bolts for the Social Sciences* (Cambridge: Cambridge University Press, 1989), by Jon Elster, a very readable account of prominent causal mechanisms used in social scientific explanation.
3. The studies on which this example is based describe the situation as it existed before a vaccine for hepatitis B was developed. It is interesting to note that before the

advent of the vaccine, the chances of dying from accidental exposure to hepatitis B were almost identical to those today associated with accidental exposure to HIV. Yet the hepatitis B risk received much less attention than that given today to accidental HIV exposure in the medical community.

4. From *Experiments in the Generation of Insects*, by Francisco Redi, translated from the 1688 Italian edition by Mab Bigelow (Chicago: The Open Court Publishing Company, 1909).

5. *Test Your ESP*, edited by Martin Ebon (New York: Signet, 1970), p. 73.

6. Editorial by David Sarasohn, *The Oregonian*, October 3, 1991. Copyright © 1991 Oregonian Publishing Co.

7. Adapted from a case study in *Rival Hypotheses*, by Schuyler W. Huck and Howard M. Sandler (New York: Harper & Row, 1976).

3

Establishing Causal Links

Causes and Explanations

In Chapter 2, we noted that one important kind of explanation is explanation by reference to causal factors. Recall one of our examples: Money appears under a child's pillow on the morning after he or she has carefully placed a recently lost tooth there. Why? Because the child's parents removed the tooth and substituted the money while the child was sleeping. When we explain by giving the cause or causes of a thing, we normally assume a link between the causes we give and their effect. Thus, in our example, the actions of the parents can explain the phenomenon in question precisely because of the obvious connection between the two. Even if our explanation turned out to be wrong (maybe somebody else put the money under the pillow), there is little question of the link between the explanation and the phenomenon explained: If the parents had placed the money under the pillow, that would account for why it was there the next morning.

Often, scientific research is motivated by an interest not simply in giving causal explanations where the causal link is clear, but in establishing new causal links. Consider some examples where what is at issue is the causal link itself: (1) Recent studies show that the French have much lower rates of heart disease than Americans do. One major difference between French and American diets is that the French consume much more red wine. (2) Several years ago, a number of dentists claimed that certain ailments, among them chronic fatigue, resulted from the gradual release into the body of mercury used in dental fillings. (3) Many environmental scientists today contend that chlorofluorocarbons released into the atmosphere are depleting the ozone layer.

In all of these examples, a claim is made about a suspected causal link. In the first, it is between red wine consumption and heart disease; in the second, between the mercury in fillings and chronic fatigue; in our final example, the suspected causal link is between the increased amounts of fluorocarbons introduced into the atmosphere and the depletion of the ozone layer.

Causal research is also prompted by the discovery of puzzling phenomena, the possible causes of which are unknown: (1) Over the past two decades, Scholastic Aptitude Test (SAT) scores have decreased significantly nationwide. Why? What factors have brought this about? Suppose we have a hunch that one important factor might be the amount of television students watch. Is television viewing a contributing factor? (2) Psychologists have long suspected that the workplace environment can affect worker productivity. But what specific factors contribute to increased productivity? Imagine we have spent some time observing workers in a large office where productivity has diminished over the past months. At the same time, the company has expanded, with the net effect that the office is clearly overcrowded. Could overcrowding be the cause of decreased productivity?

All our examples make new and interesting claims about possible causal links. But how do we go about determining whether such claims are true? Our task in this chapter is to look at the way in which causal links are established. The method we will examine is a variation of the method for testing explanations introduced in Chapter 2. In Chapter 2 we were concerned with the design of experiments intended to test explanations. Here we will be concerned with experiments and studies designed to provide evidence for causal links. That the two methods should be slightly different is suggested by a point made in our discussion of various types of explanation at the beginning of Chapter 2: To establish a causal link is but a preliminary step in the process of explanation. Presuming we have established a link, say, between television viewing and SAT scores, our work has only just begun. Our next task would be to attempt to get at the causal mechanism by which television viewing acts on SAT scores. Is it simply that time that used to be spent studying is now spent watching television? Does prolonged television viewing somehow decrease one's ability to study or to take tests like the SAT? The point here can be simply put: It is one thing to establish a causal link, but quite another to explain why the link should hold.

Causes and Correlations

Before we turn to the question of how causal links are established, we must distinguish between two closely related kinds of claims that frequently occur in discussions of causation. You have probably heard the dictum "Correlation is not causation." More precisely, to establish a correlation between two things is not to establish any sort of causal link between them. A *corre-*

lation is a simple statistical comparison between a pair of characteristics or factors. To say that there is a correlation between two characteristics, X and Y, is simply to say that Y occurs with a different frequency among things having X than among things not having X. Correlations can be positive or negative. If I assert, for example, that there is a *positive correlation* between marijuana use and heroin use, I am merely claiming that a higher percentage of marijuana users than non–marijuana users also use heroin. If I assert that fewer alcoholics than nonalcoholics use marijuana, I am claiming a *negative correlation* between marijuana use and alcoholism.

That correlation is not causation is shown by the following case. Suppose we were to discover this rather interesting relationship: Americans who watch little or no televised football consume much less beer, on average, than do Americans who watch a great deal of football. Here we have a strong positive correlation between watching football on TV and beer consumption, yet we have, on the basis of the relationship we have uncovered, no reason to suspect that the two factors are causally related. It is entirely possible we have uncovered nothing more than a coincidence, a "mere correlation." It is also possible that some other factor is responsible for the correlation. If, for example, American males drink more beer than American females and if males watch more football on TV than do females, then the correlation may be noncoincidental, yet still not evidence that watching football on TV is responsible for increased beer consumption.

All of this is not to say that there can be no causal link between two correlated factors. Indeed, if two factors, A and B, are causally linked, they will be correlated. But the simple fact that two factors are correlated, by itself, provides no evidence for a causal link. To make a case for a causal link between two factors, we would need to establish that the first factor is responsible for the second. And this brings us to our main topic: the method by which causal links are established.

An Ideal Test

I've invented a new flea collar for dogs; it's made of organically grown substances—herbs and the like—not synthetic chemicals. I call it the "Nature's Own Way" flea collar, or NOW for short, and I'm sure there is a market for NOW, given current concerns with the environment and utilizing natural substances. But I have one small question that needs to be answered before putting the NOW collar on the market: Do NOW collars work? Will my new flea collar actually eliminate fleas? To decide this question, we might perform the following test.

First, we need subjects—a considerable number of dogs, of all breeds, with a considerable number of fleas. So let's borrow, say, 500 experimental subjects from local animal shelters. Next, we will hire a veterinarian and instruct him or her to screen our 500 subjects, eliminating all but the 200 with the most fleas. Then, using a random procedure, we will divide the dogs into two groups: We will assign each dog a number, put the numbers in a hat, and select at random two subgroups of 100 dogs each. After isolating the two groups from one another, we will board them in identical environments. Now comes the crucial step. We will put NOW collars on the subjects in the first subgroup, but not on those in second group. After two weeks, we will have our veterinarian examine each dog for fleas.

Suppose that the results are as follows: All the dogs in group 1 are virtually free of fleas, while all those in group 2 are riddled with fleas. These results would certainly indicate that NOW collars work—that there is a definite causal link between the use of NOW collars and the eradication of fleas.

What we have just illustrated is the basic strategy followed in designing and carrying out causal experiments—experiments designed to detect causal links. We begin with a claim about a purported causal link, often called a *causal hypothesis*—say, "A causes B." Normally, causal hypotheses will be claims about groups, not about single individuals. In effect, then, "A causes B" really means "A causes B in subjects of type C." The subjects studied in causal experiments will often be people but, as our illustration suggests, can be just about anything. Next we select a limited number of Cs and divide them into two groups of equal size. It is crucial that we select Cs that are alike with respect to any factor, other than A, that we suspect might be a cause of B. Our interest, then, is in working with a group in which, if B appears in one group but not the other, the most reasonable explanation would be the introduction of A. The first group is called the *experimental group* (EG) and the second, the *control group* (CG). The control group is aptly named, for it provides a benchmark by which to judge whether the level of the effect manifested in the experimental group is actually a product of the suspected causal agent.

Finally, we administer the suspected causal agent, A, to the subjects in EG but not to those in CG, and await results. (In the jargon of the causal researcher, the suspected causal agent is sometimes called the *independent variable* and the effect, the *dependent variable*.) If, after the appropriate amount of time has elapsed, only members of EG have B, we conclude that A causes B in Cs. But if the subjects in EG do not have B, we conclude that A does not cause B in Cs.

We can set this process out as a series of steps:

1. Begin with a causal hypothesis: A causes B in Cs.
2. Select a representative group of Cs, all of whom are alike with respect to any factor, other than A, that might cause B.
3. Divide the representative group into two subgroups, called the *experimental group* and the *control group*.
4. Administer the suspected causal agent, A, to members of the experimental group only.
5. Wait for the appropriate amount of time.
6. Draw the following conclusions, depending on the results of the test:

a. If only members of the experimental group have B, the hypothesis is correct: A causes B in Cs.
b. If members of neither group has B, the hypothesis is wrong: A does not cause B in Cs.

Ideally, a test of this sort would provide us with decisive evidence for the truth or falsity of a causal hypothesis. The reason for this should be clear. If we can work with an entirely homogeneous group of experimental and control subjects, and if we can be certain that the only difference between the two is that the experimental group has been exposed to the suspected cause, then we can be equally certain of our results. That is, if all of our Cs are identical in all relevant respects, and if at the end of the test all of those—and only those—in the experimental group of Cs have B, it would seem that A is the cause of B. However, as I'm sure you are now quite aware, we do not live in an ideal world. Though our discussion of an ideal test has provided us with a sense of what it takes to establish a causal link, it also ignores some very important real-world problems with which causal researchers must contend.

A moment's reflection reveals that even in our imagined experiment, lots of things could happen to render our conclusion questionable. In fact, no flea collar is able to eliminate all fleas, and some breeds of dogs are more susceptible to fleas than others. Indeed, it may well be that particular dogs of a given breed are more susceptible to fleas than others. Thus, in an actual experiment, it is unlikely we will be able to achieve either the level of control nor the kind of "all or nothing" results described in our ideal test. Consider, next, some of the problems that must be confronted in carrying out an actual causal experiment.

Mitigating Circumstances

Three important facts about causes and their effects account for most of the difficulties encountered in establishing causal links. The first is that, for most causal factors, the level of the effect will be limited. Thus, to say that A causes B in Cs is not to say that all Cs exposed to A will have B. The second is that most effects are not associated with a single causal factor. Factors other than A may cause B in Cs even when A is clearly a cause of B in Cs. The third is that factors stemming from the design of the experiment may contribute to the level of effect observed in the experiment. A may appear to cause B in Cs when, in fact, the appearance of the causal link has more to do with the expectations of the experimenters or the experimental subjects than with the introduction of A. Let's consider each of these points, the difficulties they suggest, and ways of dealing with them.

For most causal factors, the level of effect will be limited.   We have all heard the claim that cigarette smoking causes lung cancer. However, this does not mean that all cigarette smokers will contract lung cancer, nor even that all who smoke excessively for a long period of time will contract lung cancer. What extensive studies have shown is that more smokers than non-smokers, and more heavy smokers than light smokers, will contract lung cancer. In an experiment designed to determine whether A causes B in Cs, we would thus expect to find a difference in the level of B in the experimental and control groups. Ideally, it would be nice if we could predict in advance of our experiment precisely the level of difference we expect to get if there is a causal link between A and B. But this is not always possible. When the first studies of smoking and its effects were undertaken, researchers really had no clear idea of what the level of lung cancer in smokers might be. In part, early research was designed just to determine this.

However, we can say something in advance of an experiment about the level of difference required to establish that there is a causal link between A and B. But first, we need to discuss a crucial procedure implicit in all causal research: taking samples from large populations. Consider again the claim: A causes B in Cs. If C refers to some large population, such as human beings or domestic dogs, our experimental and control groups will obviously contain only a minute fraction of the members of that population. Yet the conclusion drawn in a causal study is not that A does or does not cause B in the Cs we have studied; rather, the conclusion we will draw is that A does or does not cause B in Cs generally. The reason is that we treat our two groups as samples of the larger population composed of all Cs. So, for example, if a carefully controlled study were to show that 25% of the heavy smokers in the study contracted lung cancer, we would conclude that about 25% of *all* heavy smokers will contract lung cancer.

The "about" in the last sentence is crucial. Though a properly taken sample can provide us with some sense of what is the case in a larger population, such a sample will normally provide us with only a good approximation. A question we would naturally want to ask about the result just stated is: Given that 25% of the sampled smokers contracted lung cancer, just how confident should we be that about 25% of all heavy smokers will contract lung cancer, and how much variance from 25% is close enough to constitute "about" 25%? The answer to this rather long-winded question is: It depends. More precisely, it depends on the size of our sample. To see the connection between sample size and sample accuracy, consider a simple example.

Imagine we have before us a huge bag we know is filled with thousands of Ping-Pong balls of two colors, red and blue. We also know that exactly half the balls are blue and half red. Suppose now that we take a random sample from the bag, but a very small sample: We select two balls. What are the chances that the ratio of blue to red balls in our sample will match the ratio in the bag? All of the possible results are listed in Table 3.1.

Table 3.1 tells us that in exactly half of our possible sampling outcomes (Rows 2 and 3), the ratio in our sample will match that in our population. Thus, we can say that if we actually took a sample of this size, chances are 2

Table 3.1

Selection:	1	2	Row
	R	R	1
	R	B	2
	B	R	3
	B	B	4

in 4, or 50%, that our sample ratio would match exactly the ratio in the population.

Now, let's expand our sample slightly. Table 3.2 shows the possible results for a sample of four.

Table 3.2

Selection:	1	2	3	4	Row
	R	R	R	R	1
	R	B	R	R	2
	B	R	R	R	3
	B	B	R	R	4
	R	R	B	R	5
	R	B	B	R	6
	B	R	B	R	7
	B	B	B	R	8
	R	R	R	B	9
	R	B	R	B	10
	B	R	R	B	11
	B	B	R	B	12
	R	R	B	B	13
	R	B	B	B	14
	B	R	B	B	15
	B	B	B	B	16

Note that in Table 3.2 we have four times as many rows as in Table 3.1. This is because we are now considering all possible outcomes from Table 3.1 when the third selection is red plus all outcomes from Table 3.1 when the third selection is blue (rows 1–4 plus rows 5–8). This gives us eight rows and accounts for all possible outcomes for a sample of three balls. To account for the fourth selection, we must again double the number of rows: Rows 1–8 are all the three-selection results when the fourth selection is red; rows 9–16 are the same three-selection results when the fourth selection is blue.

But something rather curious has happened in our larger sample. First, the chances of getting a sample ratio that matches the ratio in the population have decreased. The ratio in our population, we know, is half red and half blue. But if we count the rows in Table 3.2 in which there are exactly two red and two blue balls, we find that only 6 out of 16, or 37.5%, of the rows contain this ratio (rows 4, 6, 7, 10, 11, and 13). Remember, in our first sample—a sample of two—50% of the possible outcomes matched the ratio in the population. However, in our larger sample, something good has happened as well. Though our chances of getting the exact ratio have diminished, the chances of getting a sample ratio close to the ratio in the population have increased! Now 14 of our 16 rows contain either one, two, or three red balls (rows 2–15), while only two rows (rows 1 and 16) contain four red balls or none. This, of course, is better than our first, smaller sample, in which fully 50% of the possible outcomes contained all or no red balls.

These two samples illustrate an important point about what happens when sample size increases. As the sample grows in size, the chances increase of getting a ratio in the sample that is very close to the ratio in the population. Our first, very small sample makes it look as though the chances of exactly matching the population ratio in the sample are greater in small samples. But this holds true only in those special cases where the population ratio matches a possible sample outcome. As we discovered, if the frequency of a characteristic in a population is 50%, we stand a 1-in-2 chance of matching the ratio in a sample of consisting of two selections. However, consider what happens to our example if the ratio of blue to red balls in the population is, say, 73% to 27%: No sample of less than 100 can exactly match the population ratio. In general, then, the larger the sample, the greater our chances of getting a ratio close to that in the population; however, as sample size increases, chances of getting an exact match between sample and population frequencies decrease.

If, for example, we were to take a sample of 100 Ping-Pong balls from our bag (once again, let's set the ratio of red to blue in our bag at half and half), we would find that fully 95% of all possible sample outcomes would contain between 40 and 60 red balls, though only about 8% of the possible outcomes would contain exactly 50 red balls. Similarly, if we were to take a sample of 1000 balls, 95% of our possible outcomes would contain between 470 and 530 red balls, though something less than 3% of the possible outcomes would contain exactly 500 red balls. Table 3.3 gives similar information for a number of sample sizes taken from a population, like our bag of Ping-Pong balls, in which the ratio of a given characteristic in the population is exactly 50%—that is, half the members of the population have the characteristic, and half do not.

Now let's reverse our thinking a bit. Suppose that we have before us a huge bag of blue and red Ping-Pong balls, but that we do not know the ratio in the bag of blue to red balls. Let's take a sample from the bag, at random, of 1000 balls. We discover that exactly 500 of the balls are red,

Table 3.3

Sample Size	Interval Containing 95% of All Possible Sample Outcomes
25	7–18
50	18–32
100	40–60
250	110–140
500	230–270
1000	470–530
1500	720–780

500 blue. What Table 3.3 tells us is that we can be 95% sure that somewhere between 470 and 530 of the balls in the bag are red; if we took 20 similar samples, we would expect 19 of our samples to contain between 470 and 530 red balls.

Consider, finally, a slightly different outcome to our sample. Suppose that only 400 balls from our sample turn out to be red. Table 3.3 doesn't help us much in figuring out what these results mean, since it deals only with populations in which the ratio of the characteristic is half and half. Let's look instead at Table 3.4, which adds what is called the *margin of error* to the information in Table 3.3. Margin of error is nothing more than the interval in Table 3.3 expressed in percentage points, plus or minus, from the ratio in the population.

Table 3.4

Sample Size	Approximate Margin of Error*
25	±22%
50	±14%
100	±10%
250	±6%
500	±4%
1000	±3%
1500	±2%

*The interval surrounding the actual sample outcome containing 95% of all possible sample outcomes.

Table 3.4 gives us an easy but fairly accurate way of determining the reliability of sample outcomes like the one in our latest problem. In a sample of 1000, we found that 400 of the balls were red. In a sample of this size, the margin of error is roughly ±3%. Thus, we can be 95% sure that somewhere between 370 and 430 out of 1000, or 37% to 43%, are red.

Let's go back to our earlier, rather long-winded question. We were discussing a study in which it was found that 25% of the heavy cigarette smokers sampled contracted lung cancer. The question we asked of this sample was: Given that 25% of the sample contracted lung cancer, just how confident should we be that about 25% of all heavy smokers will contract lung cancer, and how much variance from 25% is close enough to constitute "about" 25%? It should now be clear that we cannot answer this question without knowing the size of the sample. Let's assume that 500 heavy smokers were involved in the study. After consulting Table 3.4, we could now venture the following answer: We can be 95% sure that somewhere between 21% and 29% of all similarly heavy smokers in the general population will contract lung cancer.

Now that we have a sense of how to estimate the accuracy of samples, we can return to our discussion of causal studies. Earlier we noted that it is not always possible to predict in advance of an experiment the level of the effect we expect to obtain in our experimental group. However, it should be possible to set some minimal difference in levels of effect between experimental and control groups that would be sufficient to establish a causal link. We can do this by treating our two groups as samples and working with the margin of error for samples of the appropriate size. Our aim is to determine the amount of difference between the two groups that may be due to chance statistical fluctuations of the sort suggested by our discussion of margin of error. Only differences that have a high probability of being due to something other than chance statistical fluctuation will we regard as indicating a causal link. The minimal level of difference we will accept as establishing a causal link, then, will be the minimal level that does not have a high probability of being due to sample error.

This will all make more sense if we run through an example. Imagine a causal study in which experimental and control groups each contain 100 subjects. At the conclusion of the study, we find that 42% of the experimental group have the effect we are testing for, compared with only 30% of the control group. Do we have evidence of a causal link?

By consulting Table 3.4, we discover that the margin of error for a sample of 100 is approximately ±10%. This tells us two things. First, since 95% of our possible sample outcomes lie within this 20% interval, if we took similar samples 20 times, we would expect about 19 of our results to lie within this interval. Second, we can be relatively sure that the characteristic we have sampled for occurs in the population from which the sample is taken at a level somewhere within the 20% interval provided by our margin-of-error numbers.

But now we need to consider the relationship between two samples, corresponding to our experimental and control groups. In our experiment, 42% of the experimental group had the effect in question. This means chances are good that in the general population exposed to the suspected causal factor, somewhere between 32% and 52% will actually have the effect. In the control group, 30% exhibited the effect, meaning that somewhere between 20% and 40% of the general population not exposed to that factor will have the effect. Note that there is considerable overlap between these two intervals (see Figure 3.1).

Figure 3.1

	Control Group	
20%		40%

	Experimental Group	
	32%	52%

Figure 3.1 tells us the chances are quite high that the difference we have discovered is due to random statistical fluctuations in the sampling process. This result should not lead us to conclude that there is no link between the suspected causal agent and the effect we are testing. It is entirely possible that a causal link exists, but that the level of effect is too small to measure using groups of this size. What we can say is that this particular experiment has not conclusively established such a link. Were the difference in level of effect between our two groups 20% or more, we would have concluded that the difference was due to something other than the random statistical fluctuations associated with sampling—quite possibly, the suspected causal factor we were testing.

Had our two groups been larger, however, the same level of difference would have been significant. Suppose we had worked with experimental and control groups of 500 each. Table 3.4 tells us that the margin of error for samples of this size is ±4%. The intervals would then look something like those in Figure 3.2. Since there is a clear gap between the two intervals in Figure 3.2, we can conclude that the difference in levels of effect is due to the suspected causal agent.

Figure 3.2

Control Group	
26%	34%

	Experimental Group	
	38%	46%

Causal experiments do not always involve experimental and control groups of the same size. Even when the groups differ in size, however, we can set minimal levels of difference in much the same way. Suppose, for example, that we have an experimental group of 50 subjects and a control group of 100. In constructing our intervals, we need only make sure to work with the proper margins of error, which will be different in each case. Since we are working with percentages, we should encounter no difficulty in comparing the intervals.

When the results of causal experiments are reported, researchers often speak of differences that are or are not *statistically significant*, often at what is called the *.05 level*. The .05 level is just another way of referring to the level with which we have been working—the interval within which 95% of all possible sample outcomes lie. It is called the .05 level because a total of 5% of all possible outcomes lie outside our interval. A result is statistically significant at the .05 level when, in our terms, there is no, or at any rate very little, overlap between the confidence intervals for the experimental and control groups. Thus, a difference that is statistically significant is one that is highly unlikely to be due to normal sample fluctuations: Chances are slim that two groups, chosen at random, would accidentally differ by the amount observed in the experiment. Conversely, a result that is not statistically significant at the .05 level is one with a great deal of overlap, suggesting that the observed difference in levels of effect may well be due to random sample fluctuations.

Earlier we noted that the method by which causal links are established is a variation of the method, described in Chapter 2, by which explanations are tested. In discussing tests for explanations in Chapter 2, we were concerned to isolate a prediction that would occur if an explanation were correct but not if it were incorrect. In a causal experiment, we begin not with a proposed explanation, but with a claim about a causal link. Our prediction is that significantly more members of the experimental group than of the control group will show the effect in question. In the jargon of the causal researcher, failure to achieve the predicted result is call a failure to reject the *null hypothesis*. The null hypothesis is simply the claim that there is no difference between levels of effect in the real population from which our sample groups are taken. When an experiment succeeds in rejecting the null hypothesis and, therefore, confirms the predicted result, it establishes a causal link, much as a successful prediction stemming from a proposed explanation provides some initial confirmation for that explanation.

A note of caution is in order here. The method of analysis we have proposed for assessing the results of causal studies provides us with only a rough measure of causal efficacy. Our method will, on occasion, give us results slightly different from those based on the actual calculations involved in determining statistically significant differences in samples. In fact, a slight overlap in our intervals need not be taken to rule out the possibility that the level of difference in the samples is statistically significant. A good rule of thumb to follow in working with intervals is this:

1. If there is considerable overlap of the intervals, conclude that the level of the effect is the same in both groups or is too small to be accurately measured with samples of this size.
2. If there is no interval overlap, conclude that the level of effect is different in the two groups.
3. If there is a small interval overlap, do not rule out the possibility that the results may be statistically significant; the observed difference between the two groups may or may not reflect chance fluctuations.

If we keep these points in mind, our method of setting levels of effect and of assessing experimental outcomes will serve us well.

In our discussion so far, we have proceeded as though all that is needed to design or assess the results of a causal experiment is a good, healthy sense of the logic involved in working with samples. But even the most precise and rigorous of statistical analyses fails to address another sort of problem with which we must contend. And this brings us to our second point about causes and effects.

Most effects are not associated with a single causal factor.   As a veteran teacher with years of experience observing students, I'm convinced that students who attend class regularly generally do better on tests than do students who attend sporadically. But as we discovered in Chapter 2, personal observation is frequently misleading. Maybe I have just remembered those good test takers who always came to class, since I would like to think my teaching makes some difference. Is there really a causal link between my teaching and the performance of my students? We can determine this by doing a test. I will teach two courses in the same subject next term, each containing 100 students. The only difference between the two courses will be that in the first, attendance will be mandatory, whereas in the second it will be voluntary. All material to be tested will be covered either in the textbook or in lecture notes to be supplied to all students. Course grades will be based on a single, comprehensive final exam given to all students in both courses.

Suppose now that we have performed this experiment, and at the end of the term we discover a statistically significant difference between the test scores of the two groups. The experimental group, the group required to attend, scored much higher, on average, than did the control group—most of whom, by the way, took advantage of the attendance policy and rarely attended class. To ensure accuracy, we have excluded the five highest and five lowest scores from each group, and the average difference remains statistically significant.

Despite the care we have taken in designing our experiment, it nonetheless suffers from a number of shortcomings. Perhaps the most obvious is that it involves no control of factors other than attendance that might influence test scores. One such factor is the amount of time each subject spends studying outside of class. Remember, tests were based solely on material available to all subjects. What if a much higher percentage of the subjects in the experimental group than in the control group spent considerable time preparing for the final? If this were the case, we would expect the experimental group to do better on the final, but for reasons having little to do with class attendance.

The way to avoid this sort of difficulty is by *matching* within the experimental and control groups for factors, other than the suspected cause, that may contribute to the level of the effect. Matching involves manipulating subjects in an attempt to ensure that all factors that may contribute to the effect are equally represented in each group. There are several ways of matching. One is simply to make sure that all other contributing factors are equally represented within both groups. This we might accomplish in our experiment by interviewing students beforehand to determine the number of hours, on average, they studied per week. Presuming we can find an accurate way of getting this information, we can then disqualify students from one or the other of our groups until we have equal numbers of good, average, and poor studiers in both groups. Another way of matching is to eliminate all subjects who exhibit a causal factor other than that for which we are testing. Suppose we were to discover that a few students in each group are repeating the course. We might want to remove them from our study altogether.

The final way to match is to include only subjects who exhibit other possible causal factors. We might do this by restricting our study to students who study roughly the same amount each week. If all of our experimental and control subjects have additional factors that contribute to the effect in question, the factor for which we are testing should increase the level of the effect in the experimental group, provided that it is actually a causal factor. Matching in this last way can be problematic, however, if there is any chance that the effect may be caused by a combination of factors. Thus, we may end up with an experiment that suggests that A causes B in Cs when, in point of fact, it is A in combination with some other factor that causes B in Cs.

By matching within our two groups, we can frequently account for causal factors other than the factor we are investigating. However, there is another way in which unwanted causal factors can creep into an experiment. We must be on guard against the possibility that our subjects will themselves determine whether they are experimental or control subjects. Imagine, for example, a student who has enrolled in the course that requires attendance but then hears from a friend about the course that does not require attendance. It seems at least likely that poor students will opt for the course that requires less. Thus, we may find that poor students have a better chance of ending up in the control section rather than in the experimental section. We could control for this possibility, of course, by making sure students do not know the attendance policy prior to enrolling and by allowing no movement from one section to the other. Another problem we might have is that poor students in the experimental group, upon hearing of the attendance policy, might drop out, again leaving us with an experimental group not well matched to the control group. In any event, it is worth taking whatever precautions are possible, in designing a causal experiment, to ensure that subjects do not influence the composition of the experimental and control groups.

In the final section of this chapter, we will look at a number of types of causal experiments. We will find that without the ability to match and to control for self-selecting samples, many causal experiments would lose a great deal of their credibility. Thus, although matching may seem to (and indeed does) involve the artificial manipulation of experimental and control subjects, it is an indispensable tool of the causal researcher.

Factors stemming from the design of the experiment may contribute to the level of effect observed in the experiment. A may appear to cause B in Cs when, in fact, the appearance of the causal link has more to do with the expectations of the experimenters or the experimental subjects that with the introduction of A.

1. Experimenter expectations. Think once again of our test of the effect of class attendance on student success. Since I am the teacher, it seems only fair that I should be the one to grade the final exams. However, it seems a possibility that I will be a bit more lenient, inadvertently or otherwise, in grading the exams of the students in the experimental group. After all, I may have some vested interest in demonstrating my indispensability in the classroom. And if you think about it, my bias here may lead me to teach more effectively to the experimental group than to the control group; in teaching the former group, I may spend more time with material that will be on the final exam. One way to avoid the possibility of this sort of bias on the part of experimenters is to insist that they do not know which subjects are in the experimental group or the control group. We might avoid the first problem by mixing together all 200 final exams prior to my grading them. The second problem could be solved by having me videotape my class presentations rather than give them in person. Causal experiments in which the experimenter is unaware of which subjects are control and which are experimental are sometimes called *single-blind* experiments.

2. Experimental subject expectations. Psychologists have long known that an experimental subject's knowledge that he or she is taking part in an experiment can influence that subject's performance. Psychologists call this the *Hawthorne effect.* For example, in our study of attendance and test performance, it is not hard to imagine that subjects in the experimental group might work harder if they knew they were part of a group that was expected to do well on the final exam. The way to control for the Hawthorne effect, in this case, would be to make sure students do not know they are taking part in an experiment, at least until the experiment is over. Causal experiments in which subjects are either unaware that they are part of an experiment or unaware of whether they are members of the experimental or the control group are another kind of single-blind experiment. Experiments in which neither experimenter nor experimental subject is aware of which subjects are members of the experimental group and which are members of the control group are called a *double-blind* experiments.

Much medical research, for example, is double-blind. Experimental subjects might be given a substance that is thought to prevent a particular condition. Control subjects will often be given a placebo—an inert substance—to control for the possibility of suggestibility. Experimenters who work with the subjects and who evaluate the results of the experiment will not be told which subjects are in which groups. The rationale for keeping the experimenter "blind" is to control for the possibility that subjects may be treated differently during the course of the experiment and to ensure that the evaluation of the subject's condition at the conclusion of the experiment will be unbiased.

Types of Causal Experiment

So far in our discussion of causal experiments, we have considered only examples designed in the following way: We begin by selecting a number of subjects, none of whom have the suspected causal agent, divide the subjects into two groups, and administer the suspected causal agent to members of one of the two groups. Such experiments are called *randomized causal experiments*. But there are two other types of causal experiment, neither of which begins with randomly selected subjects who have not yet been exposed to the suspected causal factor. These are *prospective* and *retrospective causal experiments* or, as they are often called, *causal studies*. Prospective and retrospective studies typically provide less evidence of causal links than do randomized experiments, but in some situations (for reasons we will discuss) randomized experiments would be difficult if not impossible to undertake. A fourth type of study, the *correlational study*, provides evidence not for a causal link, but for a correlation between factors. What follows is a brief description of the three basic types of causal experiment and of correlational studies along with a summary of the advantages and limits of each.

Randomized causal experiments.   A randomized causal experiment is the sort of experiment with which we have been working. The subjects used in the experiment are selected and randomly divided into two groups prior to administering the suspected causal agent. Randomized experiments are capable of providing strong evidence precisely because they enable us to control quite effectively for other possible causal factors. Selecting subjects prior to exposing them to the suspected cause and dividing them randomly into experimental and control groups both go a long way toward controlling for extraneous causal factors.

Randomized experiments, however, have a number of disadvantages. They tend to be quite expensive and time-consuming to carry out, particularly if it is necessary to work with large groups of subjects. Unless the suspected effect follows reasonably immediately upon exposure to the casual agent, randomized experiments may take a great deal of time to carry out. Does exercise have an influence on longevity? Though I suppose we might design a randomized test of the possible link between the two, the test would take years to complete. Finally, we would have grave reservations, to say the least, about carrying out randomized experiments dealing with many suspected causal links. Do high rates of cholesterol in the blood cause heart disease? Imagine what a randomized experiment might involve. We might begin, for example, with a large number of small children. Having divided them at random into two groups, we will train one group to eat lots of fatty, unhealthy foods of the sort we suspect may be associated with high levels of cholesterol. I'm sure you can see the problem. Not coincidentally, much medical research is carried out on laboratory animals precisely because we tend to have much less hesitation about administering potentially hazardous substances to members of nonhuman species.

Prospective causal experiments. In prospective causal experiments, we begin with two groups of subjects, one of which—the experimental group— already has the suspected causal factor, while the other group does not. During the course of the experiment, we wait to see any emerging difference in the level of the effect in the two groups.

Consider, for example, how we might carry out a prospective experiment to investigate the link between class attendance and test performance. We might begin by selecting a large number of students at random. Next, we must find some way of accurately determining their patterns of class attendance. We might, for example, simply observe them for, say, the first ten weeks of my course. Then, we divide our subjects into two groups: those who attend class regularly (defined, let's say, as those who miss less than 5% of all classes) and those who do not. The former become our experimental group and the latter, our control group. If we find that more than half of our subjects are in one group or the other, we can pare down the size of the larger group by randomly excluding subjects from the larger group. Now, we track our subjects and await the results of the final exam. Such an experiment is called *prospective* because it is future-oriented. We select subjects who already have the suspected cause and wait to see what happens with respect to the effect.

To see the primary limitation of prospective experiments, imagine that we actually carry out the experiment just described and discover a statistically significant difference in levels of test performance between the two groups: The experimental group scored much higher, on average, than the control group on the final. This result may not demonstrate a link between attendance and test performance. In selecting individuals for membership in our experimental and control groups, we were guided by a single consideration: class attendance. Yet there are clearly other factors that might influence test performance, one of which we discussed earlier: the amount one studies. Undoubtedly there a number of other contributing factors, such as how effectively one studies, how motivated one is to achieve outstanding grades, and how much one already knows about the subject matter of the course. By concentrating on a single causal factor in our selection process, we leave open the possibility that whatever difference in levels of effect we observe in our two groups may be due to other factors. This, of course, is precisely where prospective experiments differ from randomized experiments. By randomly dividing subjects into experimental and control groups *prior to administering the suspected cause*, we greatly decrease the chances that other factors will account for differences in level of effect. In prospective experiments, it is always possible that other factors will come into play precisely because we begin with subjects already having the suspected cause.

Matching can be used to control for potentially troublesome causal factors in prospective experiments. Suppose, for example, we discover that about 50% of our experimental subjects study five or more hours per week per course, whereas only 35% of our control subject study at this level. We can easily subtract some subjects from our experimental group or add some to the control group to achieve similar percentages of this obvious causal factor. It is not an oversimplification to say that the reliability of a prospective experiment is in direct proportion to the degree to which such matching is successful. Thus, in assessing the results of a prospective experiment, we need to know what factors have been controlled for through matching. In addition, it is always wise to be on the lookout for other factors that might influence the experiment's outcome but have not been controlled for. In general, a properly done prospective study can provide some strong indication of a causal link, though, still not as strong as that provided by a randomized experiment.

In some respects, prospective experiments offer us advantages over randomized causal experiments. For one thing, prospective experiments require much less direct manipulation of experimental subjects and, thus, tend to be easier and less expensive to carry out and to occasion fewer ethical objections. Their principal advantage, however, lies in the fact that they enable us to work with very large groups. And as we have discovered, causal factors often result in differences in level of effect that are so small as to require large samples to detect. Moreover, greater size alone increases the chances that our samples will be representative with respect to other causal factors. This is crucial when an effect is associated with several causal factors. If a number of factors cause B in Cs, we increase our chances of accurately representing the levels of these other factors in our two groups as we increase their size. In addition, prospective experiments allow us to study potential causal links we could not make the subject of randomized experiments. As we pointed out earlier, we would all have serious reservations about a randomized experiment dealing with cholesterol and heart disease, in human beings at any rate. However, we should have no similar moral reservations about a study that involved nothing more than tracking people with preexisting high levels of cholesterol.

Retrospective causal experiments. Retrospective experiments or studies begin with two groups—our familiar experimental and control groups—but the two are composed of subjects who do and do not have the effect in question. Remember, in randomized and prospective studies, subjects will not have the effect being tested for prior to the beginning of the study. By contrast, retrospective studies look to the past in an attempt to discover differences in the level of potential causal factors.

To carry out a retrospective study of the link between class attendance and test performance, we need only to look at records of past classes. We might begin by looking for students who have done well on the final, which we might define as having scored 85% or higher. We then select two groups of students: those who have scored 85% or higher and those who have scored lower than 85%. The former students constitute our experimental group and the latter, our control group. Fortunately, I have kept detailed attendance records for all past classes. So we look at the attendance records for our two groups. If there is a link between attendance and test performance, we would expect to find significantly better rates of attendance for students in our experimental group.

Even the best of retrospective studies can provide only weak evidence for a causal link. This is because in retrospective studies, it is exceedingly difficult to control for other potential causal factors. Subjects are selected because they either do or do not have the effect in question, so potential causal factors other than that for which we are testing may be automatically built into our two groups.

A kind of backward matching is possible in retrospective studies. Suppose that in our study of the link between class attendance and test performance, we discover that 50% of our experimental group spend five hours or more per week preparing for each of their classes, while only 20% of our control group do so. It may be possible to do some matching here, by eliminating subjects from one group or adding more to the other and then looking to see whether the difference in levels of the suspected cause in the two groups remains the same. However, even if, by the process of backward matching, we are able to configure our two groups so that they exhibit similar levels of other suspected causes, we have at most very tentative evidence for the causal link in question.

All we are in a position to conclude, as the result of a retrospective study, is that we have looked into the background of subjects who have a particular effect and have found that a suspected cause occurs more frequently in them than in subjects who do not have the effect in question. Whether the effect is due to the suspected cause is difficult to say, even when pains are taken to control for other potential causal factors. For in manipulating other causal factors, we may well have disturbed some combination of factors that is responsible for instances of the effect in our experimental group. That our two groups now appear to be alike with respect to other causal factors is, thus, largely because they are contrived to appear that way.

One final limitation of retrospective studies is that they provide no way of estimating the level of difference of the effect being studied. The very design of retrospective studies ensures that 100% of the experimental group but none of the control group will have the effect. Because of their limitations, retrospective studies are best regarded as a tool for uncovering potential causal links. We discover that a number of people have contracted effect B. Comparing them with a group of people who do not have B, we find a significant difference in the level of some factor, A. It would seem that A may well be a cause of B. To determine more about the potential link between A and B, we would be well advised to undertake a more careful prospective or randomized experiment.

The advantages to retrospective studies, by contrast with randomized and prospective studies, are that they can be carried out quickly and inexpensively, since they involve little more than careful analysis of data that are already available. And sometimes alacrity is of the essence. Imagine we have discovered that, say, Guernsey cows are dying at an alarming rate from unknown causes. What we need before we can do much of anything is some sense of what might be causing the problem. A quick search for factors in the background of infected cows that are absent at a significant level in the background of noninfected cows might turn up just the clue we need.

Correlational studies.   Recall our earlier discussion of correlation. We said that a correlation is a statistical comparison between a pair of factors. To say that there is a correlation between two factors, X and Y, is simply a way of saying Y occurs with a different frequency among things having X than among things not having X.

A correlational study is a search, usually within a large statistical base, for interesting relationships between pairs of factors. In a correlational study of a population of Cs, we might discover that more Cs who have A than Cs who do not have A also have B. What this shows is a positive correlation between A and B in Cs. So, for example, imagine we have examined records for a number of my past classes and have discovered that more students who attend class regularly than students who attend sporadically have done well on the final exam. This indicates a positive correlation between class attendance and test performance for students enrolled in my classes.

A correlational study does not establish a causal link between the features correlated. Suppose, for example, we looked at the birth dates of students enrolled in my last class and discovered that about half were born in one of the first six months of the year. Imagine we also discovered that more than half of all high test scores were achieved by students in this group. What this means is that there is a correlation between being born in the first half of the year and superior test performance. Yet it seems highly unlikely that there is a causal relationship between the two. As in retrospective studies, the real value of correlational studies lies in the fact that they provide a quick and easy way of discovering possible causal links. Absent any additional evidence that a correlation involves a causal link, however, we must regard the results of a correlational study as having established a correlation between two factors, and nothing more. The distinction between causation and correlation is sometimes lost in media reports of correlational studies. Beware of stories that claim a "link," "connection," or "tie" between two factors when really all that is being reported on is a correlational study.

Summary

Let's see if we can reduce our findings about causes and effects and various types of causal experiments to a bare minimum. First, here are brief definitions of some technical terms that come up frequently in discussions of causal experiments:

Causal study: just another name for a causal experiment.

Causal hypothesis: just another name for a claim of a causal link.

Matching: altering the composition of experimental or control groups to account for causal factors not under investigation.

Null hypothesis: the claim that there is no difference in levels of effect in the populations corresponding to the two experimental samples.

Single-blind: an experiment in which either the experimenters or experimental subjects are intentionally deprived of certain information about the experiment. Typically, information will be withheld from experimenters or experimental subjects about which subjects are in which groups.

Double-blind: an experiment in which both experimenters and experimental subjects are intentionally deprived of information.

Margin of error: an interval around a sample outcome wherein a certain percentage of possible sample outcomes lie. In much causal research, the interval used contains 95% of all possible sample outcomes.

Statistically significant difference: a difference in sample outcomes that is highly unlikely to be due to normal sample fluctuations.

Causal experiments are of four distinct types. Here is a brief description of each.

Randomized experiments: A group of subjects are divided at random into experimental and control groups, and the suspected cause is administered to members of the experimental group only.

Prospective experiments: Subjects are selected for the experimental group who have already been exposed to the suspected causal agent; control subjects are selected who have not been exposed to the suspected cause.

Retrospective experiments: A group of subjects are selected, all of whom have the effect. These subjects are compared to another group, none of whom have the effect, in an attempt to discover possible causal factors.

Correlational studies: A population is examined for potential correlations between two factors.

The aim of the first three types of causal experiment is to establish a link between suspected cause and effect. Randomized and prospective experiments attempt to do so by showing that significantly different levels of the effect will occur in two groups, only one of which has been exposed to the suspected causal factor. By contrast, retrospective experiments attempt to establish significantly different levels of the causal factor in a group that does have the effect and a group that does not.

Of the various types of causal experiment, randomized experiments are capable of providing the strongest evidence of a causal link. Retrospective studies provide the weakest level of evidence and are best regarded as a method of discovering possible causal links, not establishing them. Correlational studies do not provide evidence for causal links, but the findings of such a study may suggest areas where further investigation is in order.

In evaluating the design of, or the results of, a causal experiment, we must carefully consider each of the following:

1. Is the difference in levels of effect (or levels of cause in retrospective studies) statistically significant for samples of the size involved in the experiment?
2. Have all potential causal factors, other than that under investigation, been accounted for through matching?
3. Can the possibility of experimenter bias be ruled out?
4. Can effects due to experimental subject expectations be ruled out?
5. Is the experiment clearly designed to provide evidence for a causal link, not just a correlation?

Now it is time to pull everything together. In the exercises that follow, you will be asked to design some causal experiments and also to evaluate a number of media reports of the results of causal experiments. The second set of exercises (Exercises 11–25) is important because most of the information we get about causal experiments and studies comes to us from television, magazines, and newspapers. Unfortunately, many such reports are woefully incomplete; crucial facts are often missing. However, I think you will find that the information we have covered in this chapter will help you to understand and evaluate studies and experiments reported in the media, even though the reports themselves are often quite sketchy.

Exercises

Exercises 1–10 all propose causal links. Your job is to design experiments of each of our three types—randomized, prospective, and retrospective—for each proposed causal link. As you go about designing each test, try to criticize your own work. In particular, make sure your are satisfied with the answers to the following questions:

    a. *Do you have a good sense, statistically speaking, of the level of effect required to indicate a causal link?*

    b. *Have you controlled for other causal factors that might affect the outcome of your experiment?*

    c. *Does your experimental design rule out the possibility of experimenter bias?*

    d. *Does it rule out effects due to experimental subject expectations?*

(Note: On page 65 a solution is provided for the first exercise. Look it over carefully before trying to solve the remaining exercises.)

1. Of all people who see chiropractors for lower back problems, 70% report some improvement within 90 days. Is chiropractic manipulation of the spine more effective at treating lower back problems than the methods of treatment employed by mainstream medical doctors? For lower back problems, medical doctors typically prescribe drugs—anti-inflammatories and muscle relaxants—and, in many cases, surgery.

2. Maybe class attendance, by itself, doesn't have much of an effect on test performance. I suppose a student might attend every class but fail to pay attention to what is going on. And students who pay careful attention to my lectures generally take extensive notes. Thus, it seems to me that one factor contributing to high test scores is note taking. Students who take extensive notes will do better on tests than those who do not.

3. Have you ever had a powerful urge, while watching a movie at a theater, to purchase popcorn, candy, soft drinks, and the like? No matter how exciting the film, it seems that all you can think of is food, food, food. The urge seems to arise even when you are not particularly hungry or thirsty. Though you may not realize it, you may be the victim of subliminal advertising. Here's how it works. When we see 10 seconds of film we actually see something like 240 individual frames of film. Yet consciously we are not aware of any single frame. What some filmmakers allegedly do is insert a single frame, every minute or so, containing pictures of various refreshments and a written message such as "Buy these things now." Even though you are not consciously aware of this message, your subconscious mind may pick it up, with the result that you are consciously aware only of a vague urge to purchase the pictured refreshments. The more times you "see" the message, the stronger the urge becomes. Is it any wonder, then, that we so frequently leave an interesting, compelling film to buy junk food we probably don't even want?

4. Most states now have laws requiring the use of seat belts by automobile drivers. By wearing seat belts, safety experts claim, we reduce the risk of serious injury or death in auto accidents.

5. Many dairy farmers claim that their cows produce more milk when they are listening to calm, soothing music, the sort of music we often hear in elevators and shopping malls.

6. Do you find it difficult to concentrate on a test when people around you are talking or moving about? It would seem that auditory and visual distractions reduce our ability to concentrate on a task. But is this so, or do we just use life's normal distractions as an excuse when we perform poorly?

7. Hot colors, such as red and yellow, traditionally have been thought to be mood and activity boosters, whereas cool colors such as blue and green are calming. If this is so, it would seem that the predominant colors in a worker's environment might have an effect on productivity.

8. We all know that most people cannot perform well under conditions of great stress and that the use of certain psychoactive substances can reduce stress. It would seem to follow, then, that the moderate use of a stress-reducing substance, such as marijuana, will increase a person's ability to perform difficult tasks.

9. Joggers, swimmers, cyclists, and tennis players are always bragging about the benefits of exercise. But are they right? If I exercise regularly, will I increase my chances of living any longer?

10. Clearly, a little encouragement helps us to do better in most things. Could the same be true for plants? If I think positive thoughts about, say, the geranium in my living room while I am tending it, will it do better than if I think negative thoughts?

Exercises 11–25 present reports of causal studies from books, magazines, and newspapers—in short, from the very sources on which we base much of what we believe. For each one, try to answer each of the following questions:

  a. *What is the causal hypothesis at issue?*
  b. *What kind of causal experiment has been undertaken?*
  c. *What crucial facts and figures are missing from the report?*
  d. *Given the information you have at your disposal, can you think of any major flaws in the design of the experiment and any way of getting around these flaws?*
  e. *Given the information available, what conclusion can be drawn about the causal hypothesis?*

(Note: On page 69 a solution to Exercise 11 is provided.)

11. Lithium, which is widely prescribed for manic-depressive disorders, may be the first biologically effective drug treatment for alcoholism, according to studies at St. Luke's Medical Center. The new evidence indicates that the drug appears to have the unique ability to act on the brain to suppress an alcoholic's craving for alcohol. The St. Luke's study involved 84 patients, ranging from 20 to 60 years of age, who had abused alcohol for an average of 17 years. Eighty-eight percent were male. Half the patients were given lithium while the other half took a placebo, a chemically inactive substance. Seventy-five percent of the alcoholics who regularly took their daily lithium pills did not touch a drop of liquor for up to a year and a half during the follow-up phase of the experiment. This abstinence rate is at least 50% higher than that achieved by the best alcohol treatment centers one to five years after treatment. Among the alcoholics who did not take their lithium regularly, only 35% were still abstinent at the end of 18 months. Among those who stopped taking the drug altogether, all had resumed drinking by the end of six months. (Researchers tested the level of lithium in the blood of the subjects to determine whether they were taking the drug regularly.)

12. Researchers have shown for the first time that nonsmoking adults who grew up in households with smokers have an increased risk of lung cancer. Although 83% of all lung cancer occurs among cigarette smokers, the researchers said their findings suggested that 17% of the cases among nonsmokers result from secondhand tobacco smoke they breathed at home as children.

    The report was written by Dr. Dwight T. Janerich. Janerich's team studied 191 patients who had been diagnosed with lung cancer between 1982 and 1984. The patients had either never smoked more than 100 cigarettes or had smoked at one time but not more than 100 cigarettes in the ten years before the diagnosis of cancer.

    The group was compared with an equal number of people without lung cancer who had never smoked. The researchers added up the number of years each person lived in a house and multiplied it by the number of smokers in the house to calculate smoker years.

    The researchers found that household exposure of 25 or more smoker years during childhood and adolescence doubled the risk of lung cancer. The risk of lung cancer did not appear to increase with household exposure during adult life.

13. In a study convincing enough to jolt any skeptic out of his hammock, investigators at the Institute for Aerobics Research in Dallas have shown that even modest levels of fitness improve survival. Their work began with an objective measurement of fitness of 13,344 healthy men and women of all ages; it ended eight years later with a tally of those who were still alive and those who weren't.

    On entering the study, subjects were asked to keep up with a treadmill programmed to become progressively steeper and faster. Each then received a fitness score. By the end of the study, 283 subjects had died, and a disproportionate number of these had been in the least fit group. The least fit men died at $3\frac{1}{2}$ times the rate of the most fit men. The disparity was even more marked for women; $4\frac{1}{2}$ times. Not only cardiovascular disease but cancer was seen more commonly in the least fit subjects.

    Being above the bottom 20% in fitness level was a big advantage. Further improvement in fitness seemed to have little effect. Couch potatoes take heed: Not much exercise is needed to improve the odds by a substantial margin. A brisk walk for half an hour a day will almost certainly suffice.

14. Researchers at Oregon State University have determined in a recent study that the color of a worker's environment has little or no effect on either mood or work performance.

    For the study, rooms in three colors were used: red, white, and blue-green. The colors were fairly intense selections from the Munsell color wheel, a standard scale used by interior decorators.

    Fifteen student volunteers were placed in each of three rooms doing office tasks—typing and filing—for one hour. Subjects' moods were gauged via standardized tests before entering the rooms and after leaving. The speed of work performance—typing—while in the rooms was measured.

    The researchers determined that whether the office was red, white, or blue-green, there was no statistically significant difference. Typing speed actually decreased slightly in the red room and increased in the blue-green room, opposite of what has been expected. The white, or neutral, environment also showed a modest increase in speed.

Moods measured were arousal (alertness and excitability), depression, and anxiety. Arousal lessened slightly and depression rose slightly in the blue-green room. There was no trend in anxiety. In the white room, depression and arousal both rose slightly, contrary to hypotheses, and there was no trend in anxiety. There was no impact in the red room.

15. People who overuse a common kind of inhaled medication to relieve asthma attacks face a greatly increased risk of death, a study concludes. The researchers don't know whether the drugs, called beta agonists, are themselves to blame. But they said asthmatics nearly triple their chances of death with each canister of the spray they use each month.

   The research findings were based on insurance records from Saskatchewan, Canada. The study was financed by Boihringer-Ingelheim Pharmaceuticals, a German drug company. The researchers reviewed the records of 129 people who had fatal or nearly fatal asthma attacks. They were compared with 655 asthmatics who had never had life-threatening attacks.

   The study found that fenoterol, a double-strength variety of beta agonist made by Boihringer-Ingelheim, was especially linked to complications. The risk of death increased fivefold with each canister of fenoterol. The study found that the risk of death about doubled with each canister of another variety of beta agonist, called albuterol.

   Although use of the drugs was clearly associated with increased risk of death, the doctors could not say for sure that the medicines themselves were to blame. In a statement, Boihringer-Ingelheim noted that people who use beta agonists heavily are also likely to have especially severe asthma.

16. The question: Should you be taking an aspirin every other day as a protection against heart attack? The answer: Probably, if you are a man over 40.

   The American Heart Association on Wednesday hailed new research that showed nearly a 50% reduced risk of heart attack in more than 10,000 men taking a 325-milligram buffered aspirin every other day. The physicians' health study at Harvard University enrolled 22,071 male doctors in two groups. One group took aspirin; the other took a placebo. The researchers report, in this week's *New England Journal of Medicine*, that over four years, the doctors taking aspirin had 47% fewer heart attacks.

   Among the 11,037 men who took an aspirin tablet every other day, 99 had nonfatal heart attacks and 5 had fatal heart attacks. In the placebo group of 11,034 men, there were 171 nonfatal heart attacks and 18 fatal heart attacks during the four years of the study.

17. In a dramatic and controversial finding, a team of psychologists has reported that left-handed people may live an average of nine years less than right-handers. The study, which was based on an analysis of death certificates in two California counties, is the first to suggest that the well-documented susceptibility of left-handers to a variety of behavioral and psychological disorders can have a substantial effect on life expectancy.

   Halprin and Coren based their new study on 1000 death certificates randomly selected from two counties in the San Bernadino area of California. In each case, they contacted next of kin and asked which hand the deceased favored. All those who did not write, draw, and throw with their right hand were classified as lefties. Someone who wrote with the right hand but threw with the left, for example, was counted as a lefty, on the ground that many left-handers were forced long ago to learn to write with the right hand.

The results shocked the researchers. The average age at death for the right-handers in the sample was 75 years. For lefties, it was 66. Among men, the average age of death was 72.3 for right-handers and 62.3 for left-handers. "The effect was so large it is unlikely to have happened by chance," said Halprin.

18. In Gary Posner's article entitled "Positive Therapeutic Effects of Intercessory Prayer in a Coronary Care Unit Population," Randolph C. Byrd, M.D., a San Francisco cardiologist, endeavored to answer these questions: (1) Does intercessory prayer (IP) to the Judeo-Christian God have any effect on a CCU patient's medical condition and recovery? (2) How are these effects manifested, if present?

The study took place between August 1982 and May 1983, when 393 patients signed informed-consent papers upon admission to the San Francisco General Hospital CCU. A computer-generated list randomly assigned patients to either the IP group or the control group, and neither they nor the CCU doctors and staff nor Randolph Byrd was aware of which patients were assigned to which group.

Intercessors chosen to pray for the IP-group patients were "'born again' Christians (according to the Gospel of John 3:3) with an active Christian life as manifested by daily devotional prayer and active Christian fellowship with a local church." Each IP patient "was assigned to three to seven intercessors. . . . The IP was done outside of the hospital daily until the patient was discharged . . . each intercessor was asked to pray daily for a rapid recovery and for prevention of complications and death."

The IP group consisted of 192 patients, and the control group of 201. Analyses revealed no significant statistical differences in the health of the two groups upon admission. "Thus it was concluded that the two groups were statistically inseparable and that results from the analysis of the effects of IP would be valid." The mean age of the IP patients was two years younger than that of the control patients, a difference deemed statistically insignificant.

Each patient's hospital course was given a severity score of "good," "intermediate," or "bad," based upon the degree of morbidity experienced by the patient. In addition, 26 categories of "new problems, diagnoses, and therapeutic events after entry" were measured and tested for statistically significant differences between the groups. These included such things as congestive heart failure, diuretics, hypotension, intubation/ventilation, pneumonia, and so on.

The results of the study, as reported by Byrd, employing "multivariant [sic] analysis of the data using [these 26] variables . . . revealed a significant difference between the two groups based on events that occurred after entry into the study. Fewer patients in the prayer group required ventilatory support, antibiotics or diuretics." In addition, using the "good/intermediate/bad" severity score, "A bad hospital course was observed in 14% of the prayer group vs. 22% of the controls . . . chi-square analysis of these data gave a P value of less that .01" (that is, a less than 1% probability that chance alone could account for the difference).

In his introductory abstract, Byrd concludes that the "data suggest that IP . . . has a beneficial therapeutic effect in patients admitted to a CCU."[1]

19. In the mid-1970s, a team of researchers in Great Britain conducted a rigorously designed large-scale experiment to test the effectiveness of a treatment program that represented "the sort of care which today might be provided by most specialized alcoholism clinics in the Western world."

    The subjects were 100 men who had been referred for alcohol problems to a leading British outpatient program, the Alcoholism Family Clinic of Maudsley Hospital in London. The receiving psychiatrist confirmed that each of the subjects met the following criteria: He was properly referred for alcohol problems, was aged 20 to 65 and married, did not have any progressive or painful physical disease or brain damage or psychotic illness, and lived within a reasonable distance of the clinic (to allow for clinic visits and follow-up home visits by social workers). A statistical randomization procedure was used to divide the subjects into two groups comparable in the severity of their drinking and their occupational status.

    For subjects in one group (the "advice group"), the only formal therapeutic activity was one session with the drinker, his wife, and a psychiatrist. The psychiatrist told the couple that the husband was suffering from alcoholism and advised him to abstain from all drink. The psychiatrist also encouraged the couple to attempt to keep their marriage together. There was free-ranging discussion and advice about the personalities and particularities of the situation, but the couple was told that this one session was the only treatment the clinic would provide. They were told in sympathetic and constructive language that the "attainment of the stated goals lay in their hands and could not be taken over by others."

    Subjects in the second group (the "treatment group") were offered a yearlong program that began with a counseling session, an introduction to Alcoholics Anonymous, and prescriptions for drugs that would make alcohol unpalatable and drugs that would alleviate withdrawal suffering. Each drinker then met with a psychiatrist to work out a continuing outpatient treatment program, while a social worker made a similar plan with the drinker's wife. The ongoing counseling was focused on practical problems in the areas of alcohol abuse, marital relations, and other social or personal difficulties. Drinkers who did not respond well were offered inpatient admission, with full access to the hospital's wide range of services.

    Twelve months after the experiment began, both groups were assessed. No significant differences were found between the two groups. Furthermore, drinkers in the treatment group who stayed with it for the full period did not fare any better than those who dropped out. At the 12-month point, only 11 of the 100 drinkers had become abstainers. Another dozen or so still drank but in sufficient moderation to be considered "acceptable" by both husband and wife. Such rates of improvement are not significantly better than those shown in studies of the spontaneous or natural improvement of chronic drinkers not in treatment.[2]

20. Women who took vitamins around the time they got pregnant were much less likely than other women to have babies with birth defects of the brain and spine, a comprehensive study has found.

    Anencephaly, the absence of major parts of the brain, is usually fatal after a few hours. Spina bifida, the incomplete closing of the bony casing around the spinal cord, typically causes mild to severe paralysis of the lower body. The defects are equally common and strike a total of about 3500 infants each year in the United States, Mulinare said.

He and his colleagues looked at the data on all babies born with either of the two defects in the five-county Atlanta area from 1969 through 1980. The researchers interviewed mothers of 347 babies born with either defect and 2829 mothers of defect-free babies chosen randomly for comparison.

The mothers were asked whether they had taken vitamins at least three times a week during the three months before they became pregnant and at least three months after conception and if so, what kind of vitamins they took.

Fourteen percent of all the mothers reported taking multivitamins or their equivalent during the entire six-month period, and 40% overall reported no vitamin use whatsoever. The remainder of the mothers either took vitamins only part of the time or couldn't recall, the researchers said.

"We found that women who . . . reported using multivitamins three months prior to conception and in the first three months after conception had a 50 to 60 percent reduction in risk of having a baby with anencephaly or spina bifida compared with women who reported not having used any vitamins in the same time period," Mulinare said.

The researchers corrected statistically for differences in the ages of the mothers, their education levels, alcohol use, past unsuccessful pregnancies, spermicide use, smoking habits, and chronic illnesses. All of these factors have been linked to differences in birth-defect rates in past research.

21. Women who use hot tubs or saunas during early pregnancy face up to triple the risk of bearing babies with spina bifida or brain defects, a large study has found.

A report on the study of 22,762 women is published in the *Journal of the American Medical Association*. Of the women studied, 1254 reported hot-tub use in early pregnancy, and 7 of them had babies with neural tube defects—errors in a tubelike structure of cells in the early embryo that eventually develops into the brain and spinal cord. That amounts to a rate of 5.6 defects per 1000 women.

Sauna users numbered 367, of whom 2 had babies with defects, for a rate of 5.4 per 1000 women. Fever sufferers totaled 1865 women, and 7 bore babies with defects, for a rate of 3.8 per thousand. Women with no significant prenatal heat exposure bore defective babies at a rate of 1.8 per 1000.

22. For the first time, a medical treatment has been shown to stop the development of congestive heart failure, a discovery that could benefit 1 million Americans, according to a major study released Monday.

Researchers found that a variety of drugs called ACE inhibitors can prevent—at least temporarily—the start of heart failure symptoms in people diagnosed with damaged hearts.

The five-year study was conducted on 4228 people at 83 hospitals in the United States, Canada, and Belgium. Half the people in the study took enalapril, one form of ACE inhibitor, while the rest took placebos. The study's findings included the following.

Among those getting the ACE inhibitors, 463 developed heart failure, compared with 638 in the comparison group. Taking ACE inhibitors reduced the heart attack rate by 23%.

There were 247 deaths from heart disease in those taking drugs and 282 deaths in the comparison group. This difference, though encouraging, was considered not quite large enough to be statistically meaningful.

The risk of being hospitalized was 36% lower in those persons taking the drug.

23. A large new study produced strong evidence that moderate coffee drinking doesn't increase the risk of heart disease.

    The study of over 45,000 American men by researchers at the Harvard University School of Public Health goes a long way toward exonerating coffee as a heart risk factor.

    The researchers queried the men—a group of health professionals—aged 40 to 75—in 1986 about their coffee-drinking habits. They followed the men for two years and found that men who drank even as much as three or four cups of coffee a day had no higher risk of developing heart disease than those who drank no coffee at all.

24. Running and other strenuous exercise may make many young women temporarily infertile, even though they may think they are able to get pregnant because their menstrual cycles seem completely normal, a new study suggests.

    The researchers put young women on a two-month training program and found that only 14% of them had a completely normal menstrual cycle while they were working out. However, the irregularities could frequently be detected only by hormonal tests, meaning some women seemed outwardly to be having regular periods.

    The research was conducted on 28 college women with normal menstrual cycles. None of them had ever been in physical training before. They spent eight weeks working out at a summer camp. They started out running four miles a day and gradually worked up to ten miles daily. They also spent $3\frac{1}{2}$ hours a day in other moderately strenuous exercise, such as biking, tennis, and volleyball.

    Weight loss as well as exercise has been shown to disturb women's reproduction, so in this study, 12 of the women tried to maintain their weight while the rest went on a pound-a-week weight loss diet.

    Only 4 of the 28 women had normal periods during the two-month program, and 3 of those were in the weight maintenance group. The researchers measured sex hormone production that is necessary for women to be fertile and found that abnormalities in the release of the hormones were extremely common during exercise, even when the women seemed to be having normal periods.

    If all had gone routinely, the women would have had 53 menstrual cycles during the exercise program. In 60% of these cycles, there were outward signs of problems, either abnormal bleeding or delayed periods. However, there were hormonal irregularities in 89%. Within six months after the study was over, all of the women had resumed normal menstrual cycles.

25. Smoking more than a pack of cigarettes a day doubles the likelihood a person will develop cataracts, the clouding of the eye lenses that afflicts 3 million Americans, two new studies found.

    The studies, involving almost 70,000 men and women, suggest that about 20% of all cataract cases may be attributable to smoking, said a researcher who found a link between the eye disease and smoking in an earlier study.

The latest studies involved 17,824 male U.S. physicians tracked from 1982 through 1987 and 50,828 female U.S. nurses tracked from 1980 through 1988.

In the physicians' health study, subjects who smoked 20 or more cigarettes a day were 2.05 times more likely to be diagnosed with a cataract than were subjects who had never smoked, the researchers said. Of the 17,842 men, 1188 smoked 20 or more cigarettes daily, and 59 cataracts developed among them, a rate of 2.5 cataracts per 100 eyes. Among the 9045 men who had never smoked, 228 cataracts developed, a rate of about 1.3 cataracts per 100 eyes. Smokers of fewer than 20 cigarettes daily had no increased risk compared with nonsmokers, the researchers said.

In the nurses' health study, women who smoked 35 cigarettes or more daily had 1.63 times the likelihood of undergoing cataract surgery as nonsmoking women. The number of nurses in each category was not given. Past smokers of more than 35 cigarettes a day had a similarly elevated risk, even ten years after they had quit, the researchers found.

Unlike the doctors' study, the nurses' study showed a proportional increase in cataract risk with number of cigarettes smoked.

A Solution to Exercise 1

(Note: Look the solution over carefully. If you spot weaknesses in any of the proposed experiments, try to provide the necessary improvements. Pay particular attention to the various measures taken to control for extraneous factors. It is a good idea to ask others to comment on your solutions to the other exercises. You may find that a fresh perspective will yield interesting new ideas to incorporate in your experiments.)

The causal link suggested in the exercise is between chiropractic treatment (which is left unspecified but which generally involves manipulation of the spine) and lower back problems. The question we need to try to answer through various types of experiments is: Is manipulation of the spine more effective at treating lower back problems than is treatment involving drugs and surgery? The passage in the exercise does not give us the success rate of medical doctors in treating such problems, so we must design experiments that will provide information about the relative effectiveness of the two types of treatment.

1. *Randomized experiment.* We might begin with a group of people who all have lower back problems of roughly the same severity but have not yet sought any medical aid. We might cull such a group from workers in a profession that is known to involve a high risk of back injury—say, furniture movers or longshoremen. Or we might simply run an ad in the newspaper asking for volunteers. At any rate, after gathering a group of experimental subjects, we should "fine-tune" the group to account for factors other than treatment that are known to influence the rate of improvement in back problems—for example, weight, age, and overall fitness. When we have a group of subjects who are similar with respect to such factors, we will divide them into experimental and control groups.

Members of the experimental group will be sent to chiropractors for treatment, and members of the control group will be sent to medical doctors who specialize in treatment of lower back problems. Because we know that 70% of people who see chiropractors report improvement within 90 days, we need to let our experiment run for at least that long. At the end of the specified period of time, we will evaluate the conditions of the subjects. If chiropractors are more effective than medical doctors, we would expect more improvement in the experimental group.

a. *Do you have a good sense, statistically speaking, of the level of effect required to indicate a causal link?* The difference in level of effect will depend, of course, on the size of our experimental and control groups. If we were to use two groups of, say, 100, we would expect a difference in levels of effect of about 20% (or perhaps a few percent less) since the margin of error for groups of 100 is ±10%. Any smaller difference would warrant the conclusion that the two types of treatment are approximately equal in effectiveness or that any difference in effectiveness is too small to measure in a study of this size.

b. *Have you controlled for other causal factors that might affect the outcome of your experiment?* In selecting our initial group we took pains to ensure that all subjects had complaints of roughly the same severity and that all were roughly the same with respect to factors, other than those for which we are testing, that might contribute to improvement. One other factor might influence the results. There are no doubt differences in the treatments provided by various chiropractors and in the treatments by various medical doctors. To control for this, we might want to specify the exact treatments each group will be allowed to use.

c. *Does your experimental design rule out the possibility of experimenter bias?* One potential source of bias concerns the experimenter or experimenters who will be evaluating the results. It seems unlikely that most back problems will completely disappear after 90 days, so what will need to be assessed in many cases is the level of improvement. One crucial measure of this will be the subjects' subjective reports of how much better they feel—how much less pain they are feeling and how much more mobile they seem to be. Assessing such reports will be difficult, since the reports may not be precise in any quantifiable way. The preconceptions of the evaluators might influence their ratings of various subjects. Hence, it seems important that the evaluators not know whether subjects were members of the experimental group or members of the control group.

d. *Does it rule out effects due to experimental subject expectations?* This question raises a real difficulty in our experiment. We cannot hope to keep our subjects "blind" to the type of treatment they are receiving. And it seems possible that reports by subjects of their level of improvement may be biased by their beliefs about conventional medical and chiropractic treatments. The only way we could control for this possibility would be to interview potential subjects prior to the experiment and eliminate those who seem to have a strong bias one way or the other.

One additional factor must be considered. As we noted earlier, we have as yet no information about the percentage of clients who claim conventional medical treatment is successful for lower back problems. Nor, however, do we know the percentage of cases in which such problems improve with no treatment whatsoever! Yet such information would be crucial to the proper assessment of the results. Suppose, for example, we were to discover that chiropractic patients improve at a significantly higher level that do the patients of medical doctors. If the level of improvement for those who seek no treatment is near that of chiropractors, we would need to consider two possibilities: first, that chiropractic treatment is not a causal factor and, second, that medical doctors actually do more harm than good. Fortunately, the results of our experiment should provide some interesting information on this crucial issue.

2. *Prospective experiment.* In a prospective experiment we begin with two groups. One will be composed of people with lower back problems who are seeking treatment by medical doctors. The other, the experimental group, will be made up of people with lower back problems who are being treated by chiropractors. Since our experiment needs only 90 days to run its course, we might admit only people who have started treatment within, say, 10 days, to ensure that both groups will be treated over roughly the same amount of time.

a. *Do you have a good sense, statistically speaking, of the level of effect required to indicate a causal link?* We may be able to work with larger groups than in our randomized experiment since we will only need to examine the records of existing patients, rather than recruiting a group of potential subjects who fall within a narrow set of parameters. By beginning with groups much larger than in our randomized experiment, we will be able to accept a much smaller difference in the levels of effect as evidence for a causal link. If, for example, we could work with groups of 500, a difference of as little as 8% would suggest that one kind of treatment is more effective than the other.

b. *Have you controlled for other causal factors that might affect the outcome of your experiment?* Many people seek chiropractic care only after conventional medical treatment has failed. Such people may well have problems that are, in many cases, much more difficult to treat than is the typical problem for which new back pain sufferers seek treatment. Hence, if a large number of chiropractic patients fall into this category, we would expect the success rate of chiropractors to be lower than that of medical doctors; a higher percentage of chiropractic patients will suffer from problems that have no quick and easy cure. We might control for this possibility by eliminating from both groups any subject who has been treated for their back problem by a medical doctor within, say, the last year or so.

Another factor may contribute to the success rates of the two types of practitioners that would be more difficult to control. Our subjects have chosen the kind of treatment they are undergoing, and it seems reasonable to suppose that many members of each group think the kind of treatment they are undergoing is the most effective; otherwise, they would have selected the other type of treatment. (There are, of course, other reasons why people select chiropractors over doctors and vice versa; for instance, many people select chiropractors—even as their primary physicians—because chiropractors' fees are typically much lower than are medical doctors'.) Perhaps we can control for this factor by surveying our subjects and eliminating from the experiment those with the most outspoken prejudices. Unfortunately, such "hands-on" treatment of subjects becomes quite time consuming and expensive when dealing with the large groups of prospective experiments. Other factors that may affect the outcome of our experiment—such as weight, age, and exercise regimen—can be controlled for by matching.

c. *Does your experimental design rule out the possibility of experimenter bias?* The same precautions must be taken in the prospective experiment as were proposed for the randomized experiment. Our evaluators must be kept "blind" about whether subjects were members of the experimental group or members of the control group.

d. *Does it rule out effects due to experimental subject expectations?* Our subjects have, in a sense, determined the group in which they are members, and their choice may well have been influenced by their beliefs about whether chiropractors are more effective than medical doctors. Thus, we should make sure our subjects do not know the nature of the experiment when they are interviewed at the end of the 90-day test period. Otherwise, their evaluation of their own conditions may be influenced by their attitudes toward the type of treatment they have received.

3. *Retrospective experiment.* In a retrospective experiment, we look into the backgrounds of subjects who have experienced the looked-for effect and those who have not. It may seem that the appropriate study here would be one in which we look for differences in types of treatment for subjects who have reported success after treatment. However such a study does not meet the requirements for a retrospective experiment because it does not include a control group. Instead, we might compare subjects who have reported improvement after treatment (the experimental group) with subjects who have reported no improvement after treatment (the control group). We can then look for differences in the percentages of people within the two groups who have been treated by chiropractors and medical doctors.

a. *Do you have a good sense, statistically speaking, of the level of effect required to indicate a causal link?* In retrospective studies, there is no way of gauging the level of effect because all subjects in the experimental group will have experienced the effect in question while none in the control group will have experienced the effect. We can, however, look for differences in the level of the suspected cause in the two groups. How we do so in this case is a bit tricky. Suppose, for example, we were to discover that among the experimental group, 50% were treated by medical doctors, 30% by chiropractors, and 20% by other kinds of practitioners. It may at this point be tempting to conclude that medical doctors have a better success rate. Here lies the value of our control group. Suppose among the control group, 70% were treated by medical doctors, 10% by chiropractors, and 20% by others. Suppose also that each group consisted of 1000 subjects. Of the 1200 people from the two groups treated by medical doctors (50% of the experimental group plus 70% of the control group), 500, or about 40%, reported improvement. Of the 400 treated by chiropractors, 75% reported improvement. This would suggest that chiropractors have a significantly higher success rate despite the fact that in our study the raw number of successful treatments by chiropractors is lower than that by medical doctors. Thus, it is important to have some sort of control group in order to assess the significance of the results obtained in the experimental group.

b. *Have you controlled for other causal factors that might affect the outcome of your experiment?* We might attempt some backward matching. For example, we might eliminate subjects who had a prior history of treatment if we found that more of those subjects visited chiropractors. But such matching provides little additional evidence for any differences we might uncover since it is an adjustment made after the experimental data are collected, not prior to the experiment.

c. *Does your experimental design rule out the possibility of experimenter bias?* The likelihood of experimenter bias seems low in that the experimenters will not have a chance to evaluate individual cases or to determine membership in the experimental or control groups. Attempts at backward matching might be suspect.

d. *Does it rule out effects due to experimental subject expectations?* Although experimental subject expectations cannot influence the outcome of this experiment, something very similar does come into play. The initial decision as to which group a given subject belongs to will be completely determined by the subject's own assessment of his or her amount of improvement. Moreover, experimental subjects' assessment of their own conditions requires that they compare their current status to their recollection of their conditions about 90 days ago. Such comparisons are liable to involve a lot of guesswork and estimation and to be influenced by the subjects' beliefs about the efficacy of the type of treatment they have undergone.

A Solution to Exercise 11

a. *What is the causal hypothesis at issue?* The hypothesis is that lithium suppresses the alcoholic's craving for alcohol.

b. *What kind of causal experiment has been undertaken?* Randomized. Subjects are divided into experimental and control groups prior to the experiment, and only the experimental subjects are exposed to the suspected causal agent.

c. *What crucial facts and figures are missing from the report?* The passage give us no information about what happened to the members of the control group. Nor does it tell us the number of subjects from the experimental group who "regularly took their daily lithium pills." We know that 75% of these subjects did so but this could be as few as three out of four. All we are told of the remaining members of the experimental group is that 35% remained abstinent and that some stopped taking the drug altogether. We are not told how many are in each of these subgroups. It is possible that the majority of experimental subjects did not remain abstinent; given the information in the passage, we just cannot be sure. Although we are given no information about the control group, we are provided with some information against which to assess the results in the experimental group. We are told that the 75% abstinence rate is "at least 50% higher than that achieved by the best alcohol treatment centers one to five years after treatment."

However, we are not told whether the success rate for treatment centers is a percentage of people who entered treatment or people who completed treatment. If the former is the case, there is a strong possibility that treatment centers have a higher rate of success than that established in the experiment. Once again, we can draw no conclusions since we are not provided with the key numbers.

d. *Given the information you have at your disposal, can you think of any major flaws in the design of the experiment and any way of getting around these flaws?* One possible flaw comes to mind. It may be that the subjects who continued to take their medication (lithium or placebo) throughout the entire 18 months of the experiment were more strongly motivated to quit drinking than were the other subjects, which may have influenced the outcome of the experiment. Precautions need to be taken to ensure either that no subjects lacked this motivation or that they were equally represented in experimental and control groups. Here, information about the results of the control group would be helpful. If roughly equal numbers of people dropped out of both groups, we would have some initial reason to think that we had controlled for motivation.

e. *Given the information available, what conclusion can be drawn about the causal hypothesis?* We can conclude very little, particularly because we are given no information about what happened to the control group. This is not to say that the experiment itself warrants no conclusion about the possible link between lithium and alcoholism. However the *report* about the study (with which we have been working) offers so little information that we can draw no conclusion. You may be surprised to learn that the passage contains the complete text of the news article from which it was taken! This is true of Exercises 12–25 as well.

Notes

1. Reprinted by permission, *Free Inquiry* magazine.
2. Herbert Fingarette, *Heavy Drinking: The Myth of Alcoholism as a Disease.* Copyright © 1988 The Regents of the University of California.

4

Extraordinary Claims and Anecdotal Evidence

Extraordinary Claims

In Chapters 2 and 3, we examined the methods by which explanations and causal links are tested. On occasion, however, the focus of a scientific investigation will be neither. People make extraordinary claims about things they have experienced and things they can do, and these claims, too, can be tested by methods similar to those presented in Chapters 2 and 3. Precisely why such claims should be of interest, from the point of view of science, is something we will consider in a moment. But first let's try to get a better sense of what the extraordinary involves by looking at a number of examples of extraordinary claims.

Some people claim to be able to see colorful "auras" emanating from the human body and to be able to discern things about one's personality by careful study of these "auric emanations." Others claim to have been contacted by extraterrestrials or to have seen alien spacecraft—UFOs—hovering in the night sky. Astrologers claim to be able to predict things about your future based on the position of the planets at the time of your birth. Similar claims are made by people who read palms, tea leaves, and tarot cards. Many people claim to have psychic ability of one sort or another: to be able to "see" the future, to read the minds of others, and to manipulate objects by sheer mind power. People claim to have seen ghosts, poltergeists and assorted cryptozoological creatures—everything from Bigfoot to the Loch Ness monster. Many claim to have lived past lives or to have left their bodies during near-death encounters. Others claim to have communicated with the spirits of long-dead people.

On occasion, scientists make extraordinary claims. In March of 1989, two scientists, Stanley Pons and Martin Fleishmann, announced that they had created nuclear fusion at room temperature in a test tube. What makes this claim so extraordinary is that nuclear fusion ordinarily takes place at hundreds of millions of degrees, not at room temperature. Some linguists and psychologists claim to have taught chimpanzees and gorillas to "speak" using American Sign Language. Around the turn of the century, a group of reputable French physicists claimed to have observed a new kind of electromagnetic radiation, which they called N-rays. This last example differs from the first two in that, within five years of being discovered, N-rays were conclusively shown not to exist. By contrast, a few physicists and chemists continue to believe that cold fusion may be possible, though the vast majority disagree. And although experimenters have worked with chimpanzees and gorillas for more than 30 years, their findings remain controversial. Some critics contend that the experimental subjects are only mimicking speech behavior—occasionally giving the right signs in response to questions and the like—and not really using language, at least in the sense in which humans do.

Many extraordinary claims involve healing and medicine. Some dentists claim we are being poisoned by our fillings. Iridologists claim to be able to diagnose illness by examining nothing more than the iris of the human eye. Faith healers claim to heal all sorts of illness and disability by prayer and the laying on of hands. Psychic surgeons claim they can perform operations without the use of anesthetic or surgical instruments. The list of extraordinary things people claim to have seen and done is nearly endless.

All of these claims have in common a pair of features. First, all are controversial, in the sense that though there is some evidence for the truth of each, the evidence is somewhat sketchy. Second, all appear to be at odds with some aspect of our current scientific understanding of the natural world. Suppose, for example, someone claims to be able to levitate. This claim is controversial in that although there is some evidence for levitation—photographs and the apparently sincere testimony of people who claim to have levitated—the evidence is limited and sketchy. Moreover, if levitation is indeed possible, then our current understanding of how and where gravity operates will have to be revised.

Or consider the claim, made by many psychics, to be able divine the future. The evidence for such an ability is scant—in most cases, a few clear and correct predictions accompanied by lots of vague and downright wrong ones. But if it is the case that some people can actually see what has yet to happen, we must rethink our current view about the nature of causation. Common sense, if nothing else, suggests that if A is the cause of B, then A must occur before B can occur. Yet if the future can be seen, effects can be established long before their causes come into existence. Thus, if the future can be foretold, something somewhere is wrong with our current view of causation.

Extraordinary claims, then, are both controversial and, if correct, revolutionary in calling for some revision of our current understanding of some aspect of the natural world. It is this latter fact about extraordinary claims that accounts for much of their interest, from a scientific point of view. If we can establish the truth of an extraordinary claim, we have a good indication of where our current scientific understanding of things is either incomplete or wrong. How such claims might be established is our next topic.

Testing Extraordinary Claims

People known as "water witches" or "dowsers" claim they can detect water with a simple forked wooden branch. Dowsers loosely grasp one of the forks in each hand and point the branch straight ahead, parallel to the ground. When they approach a source of water, the dowsing rod, as the forked stick is called, will point in the direction of the water, much as a compass needle will point in the direction of magnetic north. Many successful dowsers claim to be able to pinpoint sources of water for purposes of well drilling, and some even claim to have found water where conventional geologists have failed.

We have before us a claim that meets both of our criteria for the extraordinary. First, the actual evidence for dowsing is limited. We must rely on the testimony of dowsers and their clients about past performances. Moreover, the fact that a dowser points to a location, a well is drilled, and water is discovered does not show that the dowser actually located water by means of the dowsing rod. That water was found at the indicated location may have been a coincidence, or there may have been visual clues to aid the dowser—patches of greenery near the chosen location, for example. And we have no real sense of dowsers' success rates, other than what they and their clients report. How often are they mistaken? Second, if dowsing actually works, our current understanding of the various forces and interactions operating in the world today will need to be revised and supplemented. Nothing modern science tells us about ourselves and nature suggests that a simple wooden branch, in the hands of a person, will respond to a source of water.

Our challenge, then, is to devise an experiment that will give us decisive evidence, one way or the other, about the dowser's claimed ability to find water with nothing more than a wooden branch. In designing an experiment, we need to borrow some ideas from our discussion in Chapter 2 of the requirements for a good test of an explanation. We said that a good test will involve a predicted result that will occur if the explanation at issue is correct but not if the explanation is mistaken. We also noted that the predicted result must be independent of the evidence the explanation is invoked to explain. In testing for a claimed extraordinary ability, however, we are not primarily concerned with an explanation for the ability; instead, we are concerned with determining whether a person can do an extraordinary thing. Thus, in our test, we require nothing like an independent prediction. Rather, we will try to devise a set of experimental conditions under which:

(1)   the subject or subjects in question will actually be able to do the extraordinary thing they claim to be able to do; and

(2)   the subject or subjects will not be able to perform provided they do not have the ability they claim to have.

Consider now what an experimental test of dowsing must be like to satisfy (1) and (2).

Condition (1) will be satisfied if we arrive at a set of experimental conditions under which the dowser clearly ought to be able to perform. A good rule of thumb to follow in setting up tests of extraordinary claims so that they satisfy (1) is: Consult the experimental subject or subjects prior to designing the experiment. We want to set up conditions under which the experimental subjects will agree, in advance, that they ought to be able to perform. Otherwise, failure in the actual test may be taken to show only that the experiment is hostile to the ability we are attempting to test. But if our subjects concur that the experiment approximates conditions under which they should be able to perform, such excuses lose much of their force. If a person says he or she can perform under a given set of conditions, it is hard to take seriously protestations to the contrary, particularly if they are made after a failed test.

Condition (2) will be satisfied if we are careful to set up conditions under which there could be no way for the dowser to find water other than by detecting it with the dowsing rod. In effect, what we want to try to rule out is the possibility of cheating, coincidence, inadvertent cuing on our part, visual or audio clues as to where the water is, and so on. If we succeed in imposing controls sufficiently tight to rule out these possibilities, success by the dowser can be taken to vindicate his or her claimed extraordinary ability.

Now that we have a sense of what a good experiment ought to involve, let's try our hand at actually designing such an experiment. Imagine we have contacted one of the country's best-known and most successful dowsers, and he or she has agreed to take part in our experiment. We propose the following test: We will place before our dowser ten identical large ceramic jars with covers, arranged in a straight line, equidistant from one another. Only one of the jars will contain water; the other nine will be empty. The dowser will be allowed to approach each jar but not to touch any jar. Our subject agrees that he or she should be able to find the single jar with water. If the dowser is successful, the jars will be rearranged, and he or she will be retested once. Of course, our subject will be asked to leave the room while the jars are being rearranged. As an additional precaution, no one who knows the location of the jar containing water will be allowed to be in the room while the dowser is being tested.

Does our imagined experiment satisfy conditions (1) and (2)? Once again, here are (1) and (2):

(1)   The subject or subjects in question will actually be able to do the extraordinary thing they claim to be able to do.

(2) The subject or subjects will not be able to perform provided they do not have the ability they claim to have.

Condition (1) is satisfied, provided our subject agrees that the conditions we have built into our experiment are conditions under which he or she can detect water. As for (2), it does seem highly improbable that a dowser could pick the right jar with no actual ability to dowse, provided all ten jars are identical, and provided no one who knows the location of the jar containing water is in a position to give an inadvertent clue to the dowser. Under these conditions, chances are 1 in 10 that the dowser will select the correct jar. However, odds of 1 in 10 are not that small—hence, our insistence that our dowser submit to a retest if he or she succeeds in the first trial. The chances of a single dowser selecting the right jar in two successive trials is considerably smaller—1 in 100. Thus, with our retest provision and with the precautions we have taken to eliminate inadvertent cuing, our test satisfies (2). Chances are slim—1 in 100—that the dowser would succeed because of a lucky guess.

One feature of our test deserves some additional comment. We have been careful to arrive at a prediction that sets a clear line of demarcation between success and failure. If our dowser can find the jar containing water in two successive trials, he or she is successful; anything less constitutes failure. In designing controlled tests, it is important to avoid predictions that blur the line between success and failure. Imagine, for example, we had decided to test our dowser by burying containers of water a few feet below the surface of a vacant lot. The dowser would then be instructed to place markers where he or she believed the containers to be located. Suppose the dowser placed markers within three or four feet of the location of one of the containers. Does this constitute a hit or a miss? Just how far off must a marker be before we consider it a miss? Or suppose markers are placed at ten locations when only five containers were buried and that seven of the markers are within a few feet of one or the other of the containers. How do we evaluate these results? Has our dowser succeeded or failed?

The line between success and failure can be very difficult to draw when a prediction involves some sort of subjective impression on the part of the experimental subject. Imagine, for example, we are testing a telepath—someone who claims to be able to read the thoughts of another. As part of our experiment, we instruct the telepath to sketch a simple picture that someone in another room is concentrating on. Suppose the person in the other room is looking at a postcard of a small sailboat moored at a marina and that the telepath produces a simple drawing that includes a vertical straight line and a narrow triangular shape that might correspond to a boat hull or sail. Unfortunately, however, several of the drawing's details conform clearly to nothing we can discern on the postcard. Is the telepath's impression accurate or inaccurate? Presuming we can decide what constitutes a detail or feature of the picture on the card, how many features or details must the telepath get right for the result to be a clear indication of success?

To take another example, imagine that a tarot card reader is giving a personality analysis, based on the position and order of the cards, of someone unknown to the reader. The reading might indicate that the person in question "tends to be optimistic despite occasional moments of depression or pessimism" or "makes friends easily" or "displays clear leadership ability." How do we evaluate such claims? The problem here is not only with the generality of the predictions but with the lack of a clear basis for judging them. We must first arrive at an accurate personality profile of the person in question. Presuming we could do this, what objective basis do we have for comparing our profile with that of the tarot card reader? No doubt any two sets of subjective impressions about a person's character will contain some words and phrases in common. How much similarity is required to put some stock in the analysis of the tarot card reader?

In designing a test, then, it is crucial that we arrive at a prediction that clearly spells out the difference between success and failure. If, in evaluating the results of a test we are unable to say precisely whether our subject has succeeded or failed, then our test has very little point. It certainly fails to satisfy (2), for we have not specified a result that we could rate as highly unlikely if our subject or subjects did not have the ability in question. Fortunately, however, the prediction in our dowsing test seems to be clear and unequivocal; success and failure are clearly spelled out. So let's return briefly to the dowsing test we have proposed and look at the conclusion we are justified in drawing, depending on the results we get.

If our dowser can consistently find water under these experimental conditions, it is highly unlikely that his or her success could be accounted for by anything other than a genuine ability to detect water with a simple dowsing rod. Of course, if we achieve this result, our work will have just begun. For then we will have to consider what it is that might explain how the simple movements of a wooden branch are influenced by the presence of water. Where, that is, are the gaps in our understanding of things that have kept us from understanding this remarkable phenomenon?

However, if our dowser consistently fails, chances are high that his or her successes under noncontrolled conditions are no indication of an extraordinary ability. It is interesting to note here a difficulty that plagues most tests of the extraordinary. Suppose that, indeed, our dowser fails. Does this show conclusively that dowsing doesn't work? No. For we have only shown that our particular dowser does not have the extraordinary ability in question. What if we had tested ten dowsers, and none could pass our test? Believers in dowsing might begin to wonder whether our test did not make some auxiliary assumption that is false. If dowsers in general cannot perform under the conditions of our experiment, so the argument would go, perhaps the experiment is flawed in some way neither we nor the dowsers understand. Perhaps, for example, there is an undetected source of groundwater underneath the location of our experiment that interferes with a dowser's ability to function.

To make matters worse, even if we could satisfy ourselves that our experiment is not defective and that we are making no false auxiliary assumptions, we would only be in a position to conclude that none of the dowsers we have tested is the genuine article. After all, instances of dowsing have been reported for hundreds of years; the earliest record of a successful dowsing dates to 1586, in Spain. Over the years, moreover, thousands and thousands of people have attested to the successes of dowsers in finding water. What, then, are we to make of negative experimental results, given the vast body of historical and contemporary evidence that there is something to dowsing? This brings us to our next topic: anecdotal evidence.

Anecdotal Evidence for the Extraordinary

The strongest evidence for an extraordinary claim is that provided by carefully controlled testing. But it is not the only sort of evidence. Anecdotal evidence—historical reports of extraordinary happenings and reports by people who claim to have witnessed or to have done something extraordinary—at least suggests that extraordinary things do happen. But how do we evaluate such evidence, particularly when it constitutes the only type of evidence for something extraordinary? Presuming we are open-minded and willing to think critically, what should our attitude be toward extraordinary claims backed largely by anecdotal evidence? Skeptical disbelief? Tentative belief, at least in those cases where the anecdotal evidence is considerable? A kind of scientific agnosticism? An *agnostic*, by definition, is a person who claims it is impossible to know whether there is or is not a God. We might appropriate this term for our purposes by slightly modifying its standard meaning: A person is an agnostic with respect to a particular claim if he or she believes that the evidence for the claim warrants neither belief nor disbelief. An agnostic, in our sense, will maintain that one ought to remain intellectually open to the possibilities suggested by extraordinary claims.

No doubt agnosticism appears the fairest, most objective, and most critically responsible of our three possible responses. Yet frequently it is not. Often, scientific agnosticism with respect to anecdotal evidence for the extraordinary amounts to nothing more than a failure to think critically about the evidence. Even in cases where the anecdotal evidence is considerable, skeptical disbelief is warranted more often than not. Ironically, then, the kind of open-mindedness valued by the agnostic often requires disbelief, not agnosticism. To get at the reasons for this, we must explore a bit further the notions of skeptical disbelief and agnosticism. Consider, to begin, the following case.

A famous psychic contends that he can bend keys telekinetically—by simply willing the keys to bend. Hundreds of people claim to have witnessed our psychic perform this extraordinary feat. Typically, he holds an ordinary house or car key in one hand, concentrates his thoughts on the key, and, before the eyes of our witnesses, the key actually seems to bend!

Unfortunately, our psychic refuses to be tested under controlled conditions, on the grounds that he finds it impossible to perform in the presence of experimenters who are understandably skeptical. Some things, claims our psychic, are not meant to be tested.

As with most extraordinary claims, however, there is some evidence that the claimed ability is not as it is represented. First, we have the fact that our psychic apparently cannot perform under tightly controlled conditions. Why? Consider the fact that an equally famous magician can do everything our psychic can do, but by out-and-out trickery—nothing psychic is involved at all. It is well known that people can easily be deceived by a skilled magician. We've all seen magicians make people float in thin air and produce all manner of objects out of nothing. Surely, a skilled magician could trick us into believing we have seen a key bend. Of course, under tightly controlled conditions, a magician might find it considerably more difficult to accomplish his or her deceptions.

So what are we to make of our psychic and his extraordinary claim? Is he genuine or a fraud? Based on the evidence we have examined so far, it may seem that this question is impossible to answer and that an open-minded person should withhold judgment pending further evidence. Were the facts presented so far the extent of the evidence, agnosticism might well be the proper attitude. But there is a kind of evidence we have not yet considered, a kind of evidence that stands in the background of nearly every extraordinary claim.

As we pointed out earlier, extraordinary claims are generally at odds with our current understanding of some aspect of the natural world. A principle that seems well established in nature is that one event cannot influence another without some intervening mechanism or medium. The flow of blood in the human body resists the pull of gravity, in part, because of the pumping action of the heart. Magnets influence the movement of metallic particles via an intervening medium, their surrounding magnetic fields. In fact, there are no known instances of what is sometimes called "action at a distance"—actions or events causally related to antecedent but remote actions or events, with no intervening medium or mechanism. A variant of this principle seems to hold for human action as well. If I want to bring about a change in the world external to my mind, I must do more than "will" the change to happen. In general, it is well established that a person's mind cannot effect a change in the physical world without the intervention of some physical energy or force. If, say, I want to move an object from one spot to another, simply willing the object to move is insufficient to accomplish my purpose. I must figure out some way—some sequence of actions—that will result in the goal I will myself to accomplish.

Now, it may turn out that the "no action at a distance" principle is false. It may be, that is, that we will eventually discover some phenomenon that involves action at a distance. Imagine, then, that someone claims to be able to do something or to have witnessed something that could only be achieved by action at a distance. I think it is clear that we should require extraordinarily rigorous evidence before accepting such a claim. For, in a sense, the enormous body of evidence against the possibility of action at a distance—evidence accumulated over centuries of scientific investigation—is, indirectly at any rate, evidence against the claimed extraordinary ability.

What does all this suggest about the extraordinary claims made in behalf of our psychic? The slogan "Extraordinary events require extraordinary evidence" sums it up nicely. If telekinesis exists—if it is indeed possible to "will" remote physical events to happen—then action at a distance may well be possible. Either that, or there is some subtle medium or mechanism at work that has so far eluded our detection. Thus, because so much is at stake, we are entirely justified in demanding extraordinarily decisive evidence for our psychic's claim to influence objects telekinetically. In the absence of such evidence—evidence of the sort that could be provided by carefully controlled testing, but not by anecdotal testimony or even by the apparently sincere avowals of our psychic—we have good reason to doubt our psychic's extraordinary ability. If our psychic can do what he claims, we must take seriously the notion that forces or processes are at work in nature that have so far escaped our detection; we must begin thinking about revisions to our current understanding of things.

We began this section with an important question. Given that we are open-minded and willing to think critically, what should be our attitude toward anecdotal evidence for the extraordinary? Tentative belief where the evidence is considerable? Agnosticism? Skeptical disbelief?

Where evidence for the extraordinary is entirely anecdotal, our attitude should be one of skeptical disbelief, tempered with a willingness to revise our position, but only on the basis of well-established experimental evidence. This is because a great deal is likely to be at stake: If the extraordinary can be established, we must set about revising or perhaps even overturning some part of what we currently believe about the nature of things. And since we are likely to have a considerable body of evidence supporting the beliefs in question, we have good reason to retain our skepticism about things extraordinary. This is not to say that extraordinary claims cannot be established. But it is to suggest that we should remain skeptical until presented with evidence for the extraordinary of sufficient strength and quality to warrant a careful rethinking of the evidence for those beliefs we are being asked to set aside.

The rationale behind this kind of enlightened skepticism is eloquently summed up by Richard Dawkins, professor of zoology at Oxford University:

> Some things that have never been reliably seen are, nevertheless, believable insofar as they do not call in question everything else that we know. I have seen no good evidence for the theory that plesiosaurs live today in Loch Ness, but my world view would not be shattered if one were found. I should just be surprised (and delighted), because no plesiosaur fossils are known for the last 60 million

years and that seems a long time for a small relic population to survive. But no great scientific principles are at stake. It is simply a matter of fact. On the other hand, science has amassed a good understanding of how the universe ticks, an understanding that works well for an enormous range of phenomena, and certain allegations would be incompatible, or at least very hard to reconcile, with this understanding. For example, this is true of the allegation, sometimes made on spurious biblical grounds, that the universe was created only about 6,000 years ago. This theory is not just unauthenticated. It is incompatible, not only with orthodox biology and geology, but with the physical theory of radioactivity and with cosmology (heavenly bodies more than 6,000 light years away shouldn't be visible if nothing older that 6,000 years exists; the Milky Way shouldn't be detectable, nor should any of the 100,000 million other galaxies whose existence modern cosmology acknowledges).

There have been times in the history of science when the whole of orthodox science has been rightly thrown over because of a single awkward fact. It would be arrogant to assert that such overthrows will never happen again. But we naturally, and rightly, demand a higher standard of authentication before accepting a fact that would turn a major and successful scientific edifice upside down, than before accepting a fact which, even if surprising, is readily accommodated by existing science. For a plesiosaur in Loch Ness, I would accept the evidence of my own eyes. If I saw a man levitating himself, before rejecting the whole of physics I would suspect that I was the victim of a hallucination or a conjuring trick. There is a continuum, from theories that probably are not true but easily could be, to theories that could only be true at the cost of overthrowing large edifices of successful orthodox science.[1]

The kind of enlightened skepticism exemplified in this passage is likely to be misunderstood. In response to a demand for rigorous evidence, believers in the extraordinary would probably offer the something like the following rejoinder:

Well, what do you expect from a mainstream scientist? Such scientists are conservative in the worst sense of the word. When presented with new ideas that challenge their pet theories, they just reject the new ideas out of hand rather than even consider the possibility that their accepted theories may be wrong. Were scientists to acknowledge the extraordinary, they would have to admit they don't know everything and that there may be things science just cannot explain. So, the mainstream scientific community has a vested interest in denying the existence of things extraordinary.

Setting aside, for the time being, the question of whether there are things that science cannot explain, there is something profoundly wrong in this rejoinder.

The idea that science is somehow uncomfortable with or embarrassed by the extraordinary is quite the reverse of what is in fact the case. A great number of major advances in the history of science have their roots in attempts at understanding something extraordinary. After all, such things serve to suggest that there is something amiss in the current scientific picture of how the world works. Indeed, science will continue to develop only so long as there remain phenomena that challenge received explanations. Thus, far from finding the extraordinary embarrassing, science has a vested interest in discovering and establishing instances of extraordinary phenomena. An extraordinary claim is of great scientific interest precisely because it does not fit into our current understanding of things and consequently points us in the direction where research needs to be undertaken. So, the initial reaction of the competent scientist—when faced with a report of the extraordinary—ought to be the kind of enlightened skepticism we have been discussing. The scientist's first task is to try to show that the purportedly extraordinary event has a more or less conventional explanation. Only when this attempt has failed can we be confident that the event is pointing us in the direction of an area that requires further investigation.

Description and Explanation

Reports of the extraordinary frequently blur the distinction between description and proposed explanation. It may seem that when people report extraordinary events they are simply describing what occurred—no more, no less. But, in fact, considerably more is likely to be contained in such reports.

Imagine, for example, someone reports having awakened in the middle of the night to discover what appeared to be his or her long-departed grandmother standing at the foot of the bed. This person might subsequently claim:

(1) I saw the ghost of my dead grandmother.

What, precisely, is factual in (1)? What, that is, can we be confident actually happened? That the person had an extraordinary experience is clear. Beyond that, it is hard to know just what to say.

But consider two rival accounts of what may have happened:

(2) X had a vivid, lifelike dream in which X's grandmother appeared.
(3) Somebody played an elaborate but vicious prank on X in the middle of the night.

Now (2) and (3) may both be wrong. The point here is that both (2) and (3) implicitly contain possible explanations of the extraordinary event in question. And much as (2) and (3) contain implicit explanations, so does (a) contain such an explanation.

Similarly, many anecdotal reports of the extraordinary contain much more that a simple, objective description of the experience; such reports are frequently what we might call *explanation laden*. For example, "The flying saucer hovered over the horizon and then accelerated away at a fantastic rate" tells us a couple of things about the person who claims to have witnessed such an event. First, the person had an undeniably extraordinary experience. Second, the person believes the proper explanation for the experience is that he or she actually saw an intelligently controlled spacecraft.

In evaluating such a report, we must do our best to separate the descriptive wheat from the explanatory chaff. If we can subtract out the explanation-laden portions of a report of the extraordinary, we may be able to arrive at a clear sense of what was actually experienced and, thus, what needs to be explained. Think once again of our flying saucer report. Suppose we could establish, for example, that the person making the report actually saw a bright light near the horizon, looked away to call to a friend, looked again and saw only a dim, twinkling light at some distance from the original light. Having clarified this much, we would at least be in a position to think about rival explanations more plausible than the one implicit in the initial description of the event.

I once spoke with a person who claimed to live in a haunted house. Every few nights, he would hear a knocking at the front door, but there was never anyone there when he opened the door. We agreed that a more accurate description of the experience would refer only to a series of sounds, very much like those associated with a knocking at the door. Once we focused on this new, more objective description, several plausible explanations immediately came to mind.

Exercises

Exercises 1–10 involve an extraordinary claim. Design a good test for each. Try to devise a set of experimental conditions under which:

   a. *the subject or subjects in question will actually be able to do the extraordinary thing they claim to be able to do.*
   b. *the subject or subjects will not be able to perform provided they do not have the ability they claim to have.*
   c. *the difference between successful and failed performance is clearly measurable.*

In designing your test, think about any auxiliary assumptions your test requires that may be questionable. Are there things you may be assuming to be true that, if false, might enable your experimental subjects to explain away a failure to perform under the conditions of the test? If you uncover any such assumptions, try to modify the design of your test so that it avoids any questionable assumptions.

(Note: A solution to Exercise 1 is provided on page 87.)

1. The ability to influence physical objects or events by thought alone is called telekinesis or psychokinesis. One extraordinary thing people with telekinetic power claim to be able to do is to influence the outcome of apparently random events. So, for example, by concentrating on a particular number, a person trained in telekinetic manipulation might influence the outcome of the throw of a pair of dice or the spin of a roulette wheel.

2. Graphologists claim to be able discern a great deal about a person's character and personality simply by analyzing the person's handwriting. So, for example, if you don't care enough to go back and dot your *i*'s, your handwriting shows that you tend not to pay attention to details. An illegible signature often indicates a desire to hide and escape notice. Similarly, claim many graphologists, a person who prints rather than writes may be trying to conceal his or her personality from others.

3. Reflexology is the technique of applying pressure with the thumbs and fingers to specific areas of the feet as a means of alleviating various ailments. Reflexologists contend that the body and all its organs and glands are "mapped" on the foot. For example, the big toe is said to represent the head, the little toe represents the eyes and ears, and the inner portion along the side of each foot corresponds to the spine. Some reflexologists claim to be able to diagnose ailments by looking for painful spots on the foot. Throat and tonsil problems, for example, frequently result in pain on the bottom of the big toe, whereas pain on the bottom of the other toes often indicates sinus problems.

4. Do you believe in reincarnation—that we have lived previous lives? Many people, under hypnosis, claim to recall details of past lives, and in many cases the details seem to be such that the subjects would have no way of knowing them short of having actually experienced the events in question. The most famous case of reincarnation is that of Bridey Murphy. In 1952, a woman named Virginia Tighe was hypnotized. While in an hypnotic state, she reported details of a previous life in Cork, Ireland, as Bridey Murphy. She spoke in a distinct Irish accent that she did not normally have and described her life in Cork in great detail. Many other people have reported similar experiences while under hypnosis.

5. For years, mediums have claimed to be able to contact the spirits of the dead. Typically, a medium will seat a number of people around a table in a dark room and instruct them to hold the hands of the people next to them, close their eyes, and concentrate. The medium then goes into some sort of trance, and, if everything is right, the spirit of a dead friend or relative of one of the participants will speak though the medium and sometimes even answer questions.

6. Many people who claim to have the gift of psychic power say they are able to see auras. Auras, they contend, are fields of light that surround human beings and, possibly, other living things. Presumably, these auras are internally generated fields of psychic force. Moreover, a person's personality can be identified by the color and form of his or her aura, and the colors of an aura will change with a person's mood. (Note that two extraordinary abilities are involved here: the ability to detect auras and the ability to give personality analyses based on the colors in the human aura.)

7. Biorhythms supposedly consist of three cycles: physical, emotional, and intellectual. The cycles are of 23, 28, and 33 days, respectively, and all begin at the moment of birth. During positive phases (the first half of each cycle), energies are supposed to be high; during negative phases, energy is low. Critical days occur when one of the rhythms is changing from positive to negative, or vice versa. These days, say biorhythmists, contain our weakest and most vulnerable moments because the rhythms that guide our lives

are unstable. The very worst days are triple critical days—days when all three rhythms are changing from positive to negative, or vice versa. In the first 58 years and 68 days of life, there are 4006 single critical days, 312 double critical days, and 8 triple critical days. Taken together, critical days make up about 20% of all the days of a life. Needless to say, a person should expect to perform poorly in aspects of his or her life corresponding to the particular rhythm that is in flux on a critical day. On triple critical days, biorhythmists will tell you, you should just stay in bed.

8. Some individuals claim that they can leave their body at will and travel through space using only their "astral" or "spiritual" body. This ability is often called astral projection. Some people claim they can travel, almost instantaneously, to the far corners of the world, while others claim even to visit other planets and planetary systems. All are able to report in detail on what they have experienced during their astral excursions. Some parapsychologists contend that astral projection is the first solid, scientific evidence for the existence of the soul.

9. Everyone knows that Egyptian mummies have remained remarkably well preserved for thousands of years. The reason, claim some people, is that the mummies were entombed in pyramid-shaped structures. In some way that is yet to be understood, the pyramidal shape seems to focus a mysterious form of energy on objects housed within the pyramid. Advocates of pyramid power claim, for example, that organic matter of just about any sort can be preserved if it is housed under something with the shape of a pyramid.

10. As long ago as the mid-1960s, researchers began reporting success in teaching primates to communicate using American Sign Language. Washoe, a chimpanzee, and Koko, a gorilla, were apparently able to learn and use many signs to form complete sentences, and to reply to questions asked of them by researchers who themselves communicated with Koko and Washoe in sign language.

Exercises 11–15 all involve actual anecdotal reports of the extraordinary. Assess each report by answering the following questions:

   a. *What, if any, well-established principles does the report challenge?*
   b. *Is the report explanation laden? If so, what is the implicit explanation?*
   c. *Is there a plausible, nonextraordinary explanation for the reported event?*
   d. *What should our attitude be toward the report: skepticism, agnosticism, or tentative belief? Why?*

11. Barney and Betty Hill were returning from a vacation in Canada when they reportedly saw a UFO. Then Barney inexplicably turned their car left onto a side road. That was all the Hills remembered until two hours later, when they found themselves 35 miles farther down the road, without any idea of how they had gotten there. The Hills began to have bad dreams and finally went to see a psychiatrist, Benjamin Simon, who used hypnotic regression to bring them back to the incident. Under hypnosis, the Hills said that extraterrestrials had impelled them to leave the car and walk to the spacecraft, where they were separated and given examinations. Betty said alien creatures stuck a needle in her navel and took skin and nail samples. Barney claimed they took a sample of his sperm.

12. There is a species of monkey that lives on several islands off the coast of Japan. The monkeys are often fed by humans, and in 1953, a remarkable event was reported. One member of the troop of monkeys on one island learned to wash the sand off sweet potatoes by dunking them in the ocean. Other members of the troop quickly picked up the habit Then, once enough monkeys had learned how to wash off the potatoes, suddenly all monkeys even on other islands hundreds of miles away knew how to wash off the potatoes. It would seem that when the idea reached a "critical mass"—when it was known by a sufficient number of monkeys—it mysteriously spread to the species as a whole.

13. On a few rare occasions, living human beings have mysteriously ignited and been largely consumed by fire. Although there are no well-documented instances in which spontaneous human combustion has been witnessed, there are a number of actual cases in which the remains of a person strongly suggest spontaneous human combustion. Typically, the body will be almost entirely destroyed by fire, with the fire beginning in the torso and often leaving a limb or two intact. This contrasts markedly with most burning injuries, in which the limbs are likely to be the first to burn. But in cases of spontaneous human combustion, the burnt body is reduced to greasy ashes—even the bone. There is often no apparent source of flame and little damage to the victim's surroundings.

14. In 1975, George and Kathy Lutz purchased a house in Amityville, New York. The year before, six members of the previous owner's family had been murdered in the house by another family member. Within hours of their moving in, claim the Lutzes, horrible and astonishing things began to happen. Large statues moved about the house with no human assistance. Kathy Lutz levitated in her sleep. Green slime oozed from the walls. Mysterious voices were heard, sometimes saying "Get out, get out." A large door was mysteriously ripped off its hinges. Hundreds of flies appeared seemingly from nowhere. After only 28 days, the Lutzes left their new home for good.

15. In March 1984, reporters were invited to the home of John and Joan Resch to witness the evidence of a poltergeist—a noisy and rambunctious spirit. The reporters found broken glass, dented and overturned furniture, smashed picture frames, and a household in general disarray. The focus of all this activity seemed to be the Resches' 14-year-old adopted child, Tina. The destructive activity, claimed the Resches, always occurred in close proximity to Tina. Objects would mysteriously fly through the air, furniture would overturn, pictures hanging on the wall would fall to the floor, all with apparently no physical cause. Because Tina was a hyperactive and emotionally disturbed child who had been taken out of school, some parapsychologists hypothesized that the strange happenings were the result of telekinesis, not poltergeist activity.

16. Each of the anecdotal reports in Exercises 11–15 contains an assertion about the existence of something extraordinary, if highly unlikely:

   a. Alien abductions
   b. The instantaneous generation of ideas throughout a species
   c. Spontaneous human combustion
   d. Ghosts and hauntings
   e. Poltergeists
   f. Telekinesis

Although all are quite unlikely, some seem more unlikely than others. Given what we have said about claims that challenge our current understanding of things, rate the relative likelihood of a–f, from most to least likely. Give your reasons for your ratings. Consider the possibility of prosaic explanations for the reported events, as well as the relative level of evidence for the principles each appears to call into question.

17. The following story appeared not long ago in major newspapers across the country. Comment on the design of the experiment described, the results of the experiment, the attitude of the experimenters toward their experimental subject, and the extraordinary ability they tested. What is your conclusion? Is the last sentence of the story accurate?

Scientist, Astrologer Tangle in Horoscope Showdown
By Charles R. Tolbert

One reason my family likes going to Chinese restaurants is for the fortune cookies. The fortunes get passed around, laughed at and commented on. Sometimes they are remarkably accurate, or at least that's our impression. I bet there are a lot of people who remember a fortune that was "right on." How is it they fit our personal situation so often when who gets which cookie is purely random?

Well, of course, the fortunes are written in such a general style that they can fit most anyone, but there is a more subtle effect: positive memory. With unusual events, we will always remember the remarkable coincidences and forget the times when nothing of note happened. This accounts for much of the "strange behavior" reported at full moon, for much of the "success" of astrologers and for the persistence of belief in palm readers. Because people remember the "hits" and forget all the "misses," such pseudo-science practices tend to get more credence than they deserve.

This effect is particularly difficult for scientists to deal with. When we debunk astrology, there will always be someone in the room that tells of all the times the astrologer has "read" them exactly right. No matter how logically we argue that astrology can't and doesn't work, it's hard to explain away positive, personal testimony. What we need are controlled experiments that can prove or disprove astrologers' claims.

Such experiments are hard to arrange because astrologers always say that the stars "impel," they don't "compel." In other words, astrologers don't generally make statements that are right or wrong, they make statements that are more or less likely to be true. It's hard to "make or break" a likelihood.

Luckily, we found an astrologer who was willing to make a testable claim. He said that given four horoscopes, only one of which was produced from a person's correct birth date and time, he would be able to identify the correct chart solely from that person's physical appearance. A colleague, Philip Ianna, and I decided to take him up on his claim and run an experiment to see how well he could do.

We arranged to collect the birth dates and times from a number of students in a large astronomy class. In order to insure that there was no error or collusion, we only used students who could provide a copy of their birth certificate. In addition, the astrologer claimed his method would only work on white Anglo-Saxons. Thus, no African-Americans, Hispanics, American Indians, or Jews were chosen. While he never made it clear why his method would fail in these cases, we nonetheless selected from the student volunteers only those who fit his criteria.

We were convinced from the beginning that if there was to be any useful conclusion drawn from our experiment, we had to carry it out under conditions that would be fully agreeable to the astrologer. Further, we made the experiment as "double blind" as we could. My colleague made all of the contacts with the astrologer, showed him the horoscopes, and was present for the meetings between the astrologer and the students. I, on the other hand, made all of the contacts with the students. I was the one who selected the student population to be used. I was the one who arranged for the correct horoscope and I was the only one who had the key to the correct birth dates.

After culling the students to fit the astrologer's criteria and adjusting for those who could not miss classes to meet the astrologer, we had exactly 28 students participating, split about evenly between men and women. We called in the students and had them meet, one by one, with the astrologer. He sat at a desk with the four horoscopes for that student in front of him. After looking at the students for a minute or two and hearing a few words from the student, he selected one of the horoscopes as the correct one. The letter (A through D) corresponding to that horoscope was placed on the list next to the number that represented the student.

This process was repeated for all 28 students, and then the astrologer's list was compared with the correct list that had been kept locked in my office. He got seven right—exactly the number that would have been predicted from pure chance.

The astrologer could not explain why he had failed to do what he claimed to be able to do. Our conclusion was that his claims were bunk.

Based on what we can find out, the claims of astrology are all bunk but it is not often that science gets a chance to test them in so definite a way.[2]

A Solution to Exercise 1

The first thing we need to do in designing our experiment is to reject the suggestions made in the passage. We want to set up conditions under which subjects could not perform unless they have telekinetic ability. The problem with objects such as dice and roulette wheels is that we will get some result whether or not telekinesis is operating. Suppose a subject were to attempt to influence a die by trying to make it come up "six" on every throw. Whether or not the subject has telekinetic ability, the die is bound to come up "six" a number of times, probably around $1/6$ of the time, sometimes more, sometimes less. No matter how well our subject does, we will be unable to rule out coincidence. And what if the die comes up "six" just a little more or less that $1/6$ of the time? Such results would be hard to evaluate. Just how much more than $1/6$ of the time provides evidence of telekinesis? What we need, then, is an experimental result that will occur only if our subject or subjects have telekinetic ability.

With this in mind, we might begin by contacting people who claim to have telekinetic power, convincing them to take part in our experiment, and finding out about the conditions under which they can and cannot perform. To simplify things, let's assume we have selected one likely candidate to be tested. Assume also that the subject is not too specific about how and where telekinesis works but believes he or she should be able to perform under the conditions about to be described.

Place a small, spherical Styrofoam ball in a sealed glass container on a well-anchored, immovable surface. Instruct the experimental subject to sit, with hands in lap, a few feet from the surface on which the sealed container rests. Then simply instruct the subject to move the ball by telekinesis. It seems highly unlikely that the ball will move if the subject does not have telekinetic ability, so success would provide strong evidence for telekinesis. If the subject succeeds and we have any doubts about the outcome, we can easily repeat the whole procedure.

But what if our experimental subject fails? Our experiment involves several auxiliary assumptions, any one of which, if true, could explain the failure: (1) Telekinesis does not work with Styrofoam, (2) telekinesis cannot move an object this massive, (3) telekinetic "force" cannot penetrate glass, and (4) telekinetic force decreases over distance and the distance between subject and object was too great. By slightly manipulating the experimental conditions, we could probably eliminate the need for any of these assumptions. We might, for example, try objects made of different materials and masses, move the subject closer or leave the objects to be manipulated out in the open. (In this last case, we must take precautions to ensure that the subject cannot blow on the object if it is very light.)

Notes

1. Dawkins, Richard, *The Blind Watchmaker*. (London: W.W. Norton & Company, 1986), pp. 292–293. Reprinted by permission of the publisher.
2. Charles R. Tolbert, "Scientist, Astrologer Tangle in Horoscope Showdown," *The Oregonian*, July 2, 1992. Reprinted by permission of the author.

5

Fallacies in the Name of Science

What Is a Fallacy?

The faith of most people in the credibility of science is nearly unshakable. When we read in the newspaper or see on television that there is "new scientific evidence" for X or that "scientists have discovered" Y, our tendency is to assume that the evidence for X or Y is impeccable. Certainly, the material we have covered in the previous chapters suggests that careful scientific investigation is perhaps the most powerful tool we have for getting at the truth of things. But the methods used by the scientist to investigate the natural world can be abused.

In this chapter, we will examine a number of fallacies committed in attempting to employ the methods introduced in the previous three chapters. In logic, a *fallacy* is a mistake in reasoning. Thus, if from the two statements

(1) Morris is a mammal
(2) Dolphins are mammals

I conclude that

(3) Morris is a dolphin

then I am guilty of a fallacy—a mistake in reasoning. My conclusion (3) does not follow from (1) and (2), even if (1) and (2) are true. Similarly, a fallacy in applying the methods of science occurs when one draws a conclusion one is not logically entitled to draw, given the evidence available.

We must keep in mind here the difference between an instance of fallacious scientific reasoning on the one hand, and a mistaken scientific belief on the other. Many ideas in the history of science have turned out to be mistaken, but the mistake they involve is not a product of fallacious reasoning. Prior to the mid-18th century, for example, scientists believed in the existence of something called phlogiston, also known as the "fiery substance." Phlogiston, it was thought, was responsible for a number of observable reactions in matter; among other things, it was thought to be the stuff released rapidly into the atmosphere during combustion and slowly as metals decay. Now, as it turns out, there is no such thing as phlogiston; the scientists of the time were mistaken. However, the theory of phlogiston reactions was well supported by a large body of experimental evidence—indeed, the best evidence available at the time. Among other things, the formulas by which metals were produced from ores derived from phlogiston theory. Subsequent experimentation revealed a better explanation for reactions accounted for by phlogiston theory, one involving a new chemical element later to be identified as oxygen. The point here is that both the work that established and that ultimately overturned phlogiston theory involved correct applications of the experimental methods we have been discussing.

By contrast, a fallacy occurs when the methods of science are illicitly applied. Proper applications of scientific method may, as in the case of phlogiston theory, lead to inaccurate results. But they are inaccurate results arrived at by honest investigation. Fallacious applications of the methods of science lead only to a false impression that something has been established with great care and rigor. Indeed, many of the fallacies we shall consider involve ways of lending the appearance of scientific evidence where, in fact, there is little or none.

One well-known fallacy in informal logic is called *argumentum ad hominen*—attacking the person rather than his or her argument. If, for example, I argue that every student ought to know something about science and, therefore, ought to read this book, you might reply that I receive a royalty from the sale of the book. If the point of your reply is to mount an objection to my argument, you are guilty of an ad hominem fallacy. Even though what you say is true, the point you make is not relevant to the argument I have given. By pointing out that I stand to profit if students buy this book, you attack my motives for arguing as I have, but you have not shown that my argument is somehow defective.

At the risk of committing an ad hominem fallacy, let me propose a generalization. Most, though certainly not all, of the fallacies we will discuss are typically committed by people on the fringes of science, not by mainstream scientists.[1] By "people on the fringes of science," I mean people who engage in fallacious scientific reasoning for either or both of two reasons. First, people commit fallacies because they have little knowledge of what rigorous scientific inquiry involves but nonetheless believe they are capable of undertaking such inquiry. Second, fallacies are sometimes committed by people who may well know a great deal about science but who are trying to create the impression that there is some real measure of scientific evidence for something when, in fact, there is very little. Thus, errors of the sort we will discuss are committed sometimes inadvertently, but sometimes intentionally. Later in this chapter, we will have more to say about the distinction between mainstream science and fringe or pseudoscience, but for now let's begin looking at various types of scientific fallacy.

Our discussion of scientific fallacies will center around three important questions that need to be asked in any scientific investigation:

1. What precisely are the facts of the case?
2. If an explanation is required, have we carefully considered all plausible rival explanations prior to proposing a novel explanation?
3. If a novel explanation is required, can we devise an effective test for its correctness?

Associated with each of these questions are a number of fallacies. The first set involves mistakes in making initial observations of apparently puzzling phenomena. The second involves a failure to consider rival hypotheses. The final set involves mistakes in testing explanations or claims of extraordinary abilities.

Fallacies Involving Initial Observations

Anecdotal evidence.   In Chapter 2, we discussed the dangers of basing generalizations on anecdotal evidence; such generalizations are all too frequently misleading because they are founded on memorable but atypical cases. I've noticed that when I need to do some last-minute preparation for an upcoming lecture, a student invariably knocks on my office door. What is it with students? Do they just have an instinctive sense for the wrong time to come to see me? I'll leave it to you to comment on the fallacy in my observations.

Omitting facts.   One way to make something appear mysterious is to ignore certain facts in describing the phenomenon, facts that suggest that the phenomenon in question may not be all that mysterious. In Chapter 2, we mentioned an apparently puzzling phenomenon, crop circles. Large, symmetrical geometric figures, circular and otherwise, have mysteriously appeared in wheat and corn fields in southern England. What we failed to mention is that near almost every crop circle, and in some cases even running through the circles, are what are called "tram lines." Tram lines are the indentations made by tractors as they travel through the crop fields. One of the most puzzling things about crop circles is said to be the fact that there is no sign of human intrusion. There are no footprints or bent plants leading to the circles; thus, it seems unlikely that the circles are hoaxes. It is conceivable, however, that a person could simply walk in the tram lines to the point where the circle was to be constructed without leaving any sign of intrusion. Thus, accounts of the crop circles retain much of their sense of mystery only when certain facts about tram lines are conveniently omitted.

Another example of creating a sense of mystery by omitting crucial facts involves the strange happenings said to occur in the Bermuda triangle, an expanse of several thousand square miles off the coast of southern Florida. Hundreds of boats and planes have mysteriously disappeared in the area over the years. Books about the mysterious happenings in the Bermuda triangle typically describe in great detail cases in which it is clearly documented that a boat or plane, known to be traveling in the vicinity of the Bermuda triangle, has disappeared, never to be heard from again. Yet two interesting facts are conspicuously missing from most of these reports. In many of the instances described, wreckage is subsequently found, suggesting an accident, not a mysterious disappearance. Moreover, in just about any large expanse of ocean near a populated area like the coast of Florida, there will be a number of disappearances caused by accidents, storms, inexperienced sailors and pilots, and the like. Only when these facts are omitted do the disappearances in the Bermuda triangle take on an air of great mystery.[2]

Distorting the facts.   Another way to create a sense of mystery is to subtly change the content of a factual description. For example, much research has been done in recent years on "near-death experiences." Some researchers claim that people who have been near death, typically during a medical emergency, but who have been revived, have reported a remarkable experience. Here is an account of that experience from one of the best-known books on the subject, *Life After Life*, by Raymond Moody:

> A man . . . begins to hear an uncomfortable noise, a loud ringing or buzzing, and at the same time feels himself moving very rapidly through a long dark tunnel. After this he suddenly finds himself outside of his own physical body, but still in the immediate physical environment, and he sees his body from a distance, as though he is a spectator. . . . After a while, he collects himself and becomes more accustomed to his odd condition. . . . Soon other things begin to happen. He glimpses the spirits of relatives and friends who have already died, and a loving warm spirit of a kind he has never encountered before—a being of light—appears before him. . . . At some point he finds himself approaching some sort of barrier or border, apparently representing the limit between earthly life and the next life. Yet he finds that he must go back to earth, that the time for death has not yet come.[3]

Now, if this precise experience were reported by many people, we would have quite a remarkable thing on our hands. In fact, the description provided in this passage is based on the reports of hundreds of people. But no two reports are precisely the same. The description we have just read combines elements from many varied experiences. Moreover, no single element in this description occurs in all reports, and no single subject has given precisely this description. Although Moody quite openly admits all of this, many people who argue that near-death experiences provide evidence of life after death accept this artificial account as an accurate description of the strange experiences people report when near death. The fact that people are liable to report any of a number of things, that reports are frequently at odds with one another, and that many people who have been near death report no such experience, all suggest that there may be a more mundane explanation for the things people report when near death. At any rate, the appearance of a great mystery here is exacerbated by the subtle fabrication of an experience that, strictly speaking, no one has ever had.

Fallacies Involving Rival Explanations

Fallacious argument by elimination. Suppose we know that either A or B or C must happen, and we subsequently discover that B or C will not happen. Logically we can conclude that A will happen. This pattern of reasoning is sometimes called *argument by elimination;* it involves establishing one alternative, A, by eliminating the possibility of all others. A fallacious argument by elimination occurs when possibilities other than A, B, or C are ignored in the process of arguing for one of the explicit alternatives. Imagine that I want to establish a particular explanation. I first list possible rival explanations and then proceed to show that none of the rivals can be correct. Have I established my favored explanation? The answer is no, for two reasons. First, there may be other possible explanations I have failed to consider. Second, even if I succeed in ruling out all the rival candidates I can think of, the failure of these rival explanations entitles me to conclude only that the phenomenon in question needs explaining, not that my favored explanation is correct.

A common strategy in ESP research is to claim that an explanation involving some sort of extrasensory mechanism can be established by showing that experimental subjects can achieve results that would be highly unlikely by chance or luck alone. Thus, for example, a study might claim that a particular experimental subject has the gift of mental telepathy (the ability to read the mind of another) because he or she is able to guess the playing card an experimenter is thinking about more frequently than chance would suggest. Implicit in this claim is a fallacious argument by elimination. That the subject is telepathic follows only if we assume there are only two possibilities—the subject did it either by telepathy or by sheer luck—and can effectively rule out luck or chance under tightly controlled experimental conditions. Yet this assumption is flawed. First, there may be other possible explanations. Maybe an invisible imp peeks at the cards and whispers the right answer in the subject's ear. As wild as this "explanation" seems, it would appear to be as well supported by the experimental outcome as is the telepathy hypothesis.[4] Second, even in the absence of rival explanations, the outcome of this experiment does not confirm the claim that the subject has telepathy. The only conclusion we are warranted in drawing, based on the results of this experiment, is that something quite interesting, something we do not fully understand, is going on. What we are conspicuously not entitled to conclude is that we have evidence for any particular explanation.

Fallacious inference to a causal link. In Chapter 3, we considered the kind of evidence required to establish a causal link. People all too often draw conclusions about causal links based on attractive, even plausible, but unfortunately insufficient bits of evidence. In most cases, the inference seems plausible only because rival explanations for the suspected causal link are overlooked. Conclusions about a causal link between A and B are often drawn on the basis of a number of specific kinds of evidence, none of which, taken alone, is sufficient to support a claim of causal connectedness. The most prominent of these are:

1. a correlation between A and B
2. a concomitant variation between A and B
3. the fact that A precedes B

Let's consider an example or two of each and the plausible rival explanation each fails to take into consideration.

1. A correlation between A and B. In Chapter 3, we noted that a correlation involves a comparison of two characteristics in a population. From the simple fact that A is correlated with B in Cs, it does not follow that there is a causal link between A and B. Yet people frequently make the illicit inference to a causal connection based on nothing more than a correlation.

Imagine we were to read the results of a study that purported to show a link between a person's astrological sign and his or her profession. Reading further, we discover that the birth dates of a large group of lawyers were examined, and it was discovered that more were born under the sign of Leo than under any other sign. Clearly, there is a positive correlation between being a lawyer and being a Leo. Now, this may suggest that there is a causal link between the two factors. However, there seem to be at least two plausible explanations for the data—explanations that do not involve any sort of causal link between profession and astrological sign.

The first is that the correlation is just a coincidence. If we look at a number of groups by profession, we may now and then find one where there is a significantly greater number of people born under a particular sign, particularly if we restrict our investigation to groups that are none too large. Imagine we were to do a study of plumbers and astrological sign. If we restrict our sample to one or two dozen subjects, chances are quite high we will not find an even distribution under all signs. What we will find is some entirely expectable "clumping." Some signs will have more subjects than others. From here it is but a short step to a claim about a remarkable correlation between being born under a few astrological signs and the profession of plumbing!

The fact that our study cites only one profession and one correlation suggests another possible explanation. It may be that the researchers who undertook the study have presented us with only one small part of their overall data, the part that appears to confirm the possibility of a causal link. Or it may be that, convinced of the truth of astrology, they have inadvertently pruned away just enough data—say, by excluding certain subjects—to lend support to the idea of a correlation.

The explanation for a correlation need not be coincidence nor even fudging, inadvertent or otherwise. Frequently, correlations are explained by some third factor that suggests a possible indirect link between the correlated factors. Suppose, for example, that we discover from careful observation of a number of classes that students who sit near the front of the classroom tend to achieve higher grades than do students who sit near the rear. It may be that this is a coincidence. At any rate, it hardly seems likely that I can improve my grade simply by moving to the front of the classroom. What seems a more likely explanation is that students who want to do well are enthusiastic and want to sit "where the action is"—namely, near the front of the classroom. Thus, it may be that some additional motivational factor accounts for the correlation between the two factors in question.

2. A concomitant variation between A and B.   Concomitant variation occurs when a variation in one factor, A, is accompanied by a variation in another factor, B. It is quite tempting to conclude that there must be some connection between A and B if changes in the level of one are invariably accompanied by changes in the level of the other. The problem with such a conclusion is that an enormous number of entirely unrelated things tend to vary in very regular sorts of ways. Over the past ten years, there has been a dramatic increase in popularity of country-western music. At the same time, there has been a corresponding increase in the cost of a loaf of bread. What is the explanation here? A genuinely baffling causal link? Some overlooked third factor? The most likely explanation is that we have managed to pick two completely unrelated trends that happen to be going in the same direction at the same time.

3. The fact that A occurs prior to B.   We have all had experiences like this before: Just as you think of someone, the phone rings, and it is the person you were thinking about. Recently, a repairperson fixed my furnace. A few days later, I noticed that the clock on the thermostat that controls the furnace was not working. It seems natural to conclude that something the repairperson did caused the clock to stop. In such cases, the fact that one event precedes another is probably best explained as nothing more than a coincidence. What would be required to discount the possibility of coincidence, in the case thermostat clock, would be some sort of explanation linking the activities of the repairperson and the subsequent behavior of the thermostat.

In summary, many kinds of claims are taken to suggest a causal link. Among them are (1) claims about a correlation; (2) claims about a concomitant variation; and (3) the claim that one thing happened just before another. Although no such claim should be dismissed out of hand, none should be assumed to establish a causal link. The first step in trying to decide whether there may be a causal link is to consider possible rival explanations. As our examples suggest, likely candidates are coincidence, fudging of data—inadvertent and otherwise—and possible third factors.

Fallacies in Proposing and Testing Explanations

Exploiting analogies and similarities. In attempting to explain something puzzling, it is sometimes useful to consider something similar whose explanation is well understood. Thus, for example, in the late 19th century, physicists hypothesized about the existence of what was then called the luminiferous ether, the medium in which light waves are propagated. They arrived at this notion by thinking of certain similarities between light and sound. Both appear to be wave phenomena, and sound waves are propagated in a medium, our atmosphere, much as the waves created by dropping a pebble in a pond are propagated out of the surrounding water. Thus, physicists reasoned, there must exist a medium for the transmission of light waves as well, a luminiferous ether. Subsequent experimentation demonstrated that there is no such stuff, and physicists went on to consider other possible explanations for the propagation of light waves. Interestingly enough, physicists next thought about light in terms of another well-understood phenomenon, electromagnetic fields.

This example illustrates the way in which thinking about a puzzle in terms of something similar but better understood can lead to possible explanations. But it also illustrates the need for independent testing of the explanation arrived at in this way. Analogies and similarities are fallaciously exploited when the fact that an explanation works in one case is given as evidence for the correctness of a similar explanation in another case. At the very most, a well-chosen similarity can guide us to a possible explanation; it should not be thought to provide evidence that the explanation is correct. Only careful testing can provide such evidence.

Consider one explanation often proposed by astrologers. Grant, for the moment, that there may be something to astrology and that, indeed, the position of the stars and planets at the time of birth can influence personality or even choice of profession. What is the explanation? How is it that the stars and planets influence our lives? Astrologers are likely to give something like the following explanation:

> Much as the moon influences the tides and sunspot activity can disturb radio transmissions, so do the positions of the planets have an important influence on formation of the human personality. Modern science is constantly confirming the interconnectedness of all things. Is it any sur-

prise that distant events, like the movement of the planets and the decisions people make, should be connected?

Thus, the stars and planets affect our lives much as the moon influences the tides. Of course, there is no claim here that the relation between stars and lives is precisely the same as that between the moon and the tides, or the sun and radio transmissions. What we have, then, is the barest suggestion that an explanation may be possible for astrological effects and that it may somehow be similar to whatever it is that explains the relation between moon and tides, sun and radio transmissions. What we do not have is any of the details of what that explanation might be. Nonetheless, by appealing to something that is understood and suggesting that the explanation for something else must be similar, our astrologer has managed to create the impression that something like an explanation has been given.

Proposing unfalsifiable explanations. To test an explanation, we begin by devising a set of experimental conditions under which we predict that something will occur if the explanation is correct. If the predicted result fails to occur, we conclude that the explanation is probably wrong. What this means is that, to be subject to scientific testing, an explanation must, in principle, be falsifiable. Don't confuse falsifiability with falsehood. Correct explanations, as well as incorrect ones, are, in principle, falsifiable; all this means is that they can be tested in the way we have described. By contrast, an unfalsifiable explanation would be one whose falsity could not be detected by any conceivable test. It may seem that an unfalsifiable explanation is simply true, but this is not so. An explanation that is, in principle, unfalsifiable is not a scientific explanation at all. Precisely why this should be so can be illustrated by means of an example or two.

A group of people calling themselves "special creationists" claim that there is "scientific evidence" that the universe was created by God. Some believe creation occurred only a few thousand years ago, while others believe it may have occurred billions of years in the past. Both groups, however, claim that the processes by which God created the world are "special," in the sense that they no longer operate in the natural world; the laws of nature by which God created the world are different from those we currently observe. Well, this is all very interesting. But what prediction about the world could we make, provided this claim is true? If the processes by which God created so quickly and completely are no longer in existence, then we should not expect to find evidence of their continuing operation. And for precisely the same reason, we should expect to find no evidence against the theory of special creation. It would seem that the creationists' explanation is consistent with everything that is happening or could conceivably happen, and thus could not possibly be falsified.

But this means that the creationist account of how things began is not an explanation at all! To explain something is to try to make clear how or why it and not something else happened. A proposed explanation that is consistent with what happened and anything else that could have happened instead, explains nothing. I cashed a large check yesterday and today discover that it bounced. Looking over my check register, I discover a glaring error in addition; I had much less money in my checking account than I thought. My miscalculation, then, explains why my check bounced. Had I not miscalculated, I would not have written a bad check. Thus, my miscalculation explains why the check I wrote bounced. Imagine instead I gave this as the explanation for my bad check: "It must have been fate. What happens, happens." But what if my check had not bounced? Once again, fate, I say, is the real culprit. Now, it may be that fate determines what we do and do not do. But insofar as the notion of fate is consistent with everything that happens, it cannot be invoked to explain why a particular thing and not something else happened. Maybe fate determined I would bounce a check, maybe not. But by invoking the notion of fate, I do not thereby explain why my check bounced as opposed to not bouncing.

We can say something similar about the creationist's account of the origin of things. Perhaps God created all things and did so in a very short time using special processes no longer in operation. But by venturing this scenario, the creationist has not explained why things are as they are and not some other way; the creationist's scenario is consistent with anything that could conceivably happen. Though the creationist's account is interesting, it is not a scientific account of things. Does this mean the creationist is wrong? No. What it does mean, however, is that special creationism does not constitute a scientific explanation.

So, if we find that an apparent explanation cannot be falsified, we have uncovered a powerful reason to reject it as an instance of genuine scientific explanation. As a rule of thumb, it is always a good idea to ask of any proposed explanation, "Under what conditions would we be willing to set aside the explanation on the grounds that it is false?" If no such conditions can be imagined, we are dealing with something that is at best fascinating speculation, perhaps even an article of faith, but not a genuine scientific explanation.

Many conspiracy theories seem attractive and plausible largely because they are impervious to falsification. Imagine, for example, that I claim to understand why gasoline prices continue to rise at a much greater rate than the cost of living. There is, sorry to say, a plot, a conspiracy, among the major oil companies to ensure that just enough gasoline is refined to keep demand slightly ahead of supply. Might I be wrong, you ask? After all, there have been many congressional investigations of the oil industry, and none has yet turned up evidence for such a plot. Well, what do you expect, I reply. The one thing we can be sure of in a conspiracy of this magnitude is that the conspirators are going to do everything necessary to cover their tracks, even if this requires buying the services of a few congressmen. Note here how I have attempted to turn the lack of any evidence against my theory into evidence that it is so. Thus, far from viewing its inability to be falsified as evidence that my theory is not scientific, I take this to be evidence that it must be correct.

A common tactic of conspiracy theorists is to attempt to vindicate their theories by reference to the very facts that have occasioned them. You asked whether my theory about the oil companies could be shown to be false. But you didn't ask for my evidence that it is true. That I am on the right track, I might contend, is shown by the fact that if there were such a conspiracy, we would expect gas prices to rise at an artificially high rate. And isn't this just what we find? The problem with my reply here, of course, is that I am using the very facts which have prompted me to give my conspiratorial explanation in an attempt to vindicate it. My thinking here is going in a circle. I explain P by reference to T and then claim that P constitutes independent evidence that T is so.

Much of the plausibility of many conspiracy theories stems from the fact that they seem to provide a simple and elegant explanation of a number of apparently unrelated but puzzling facts. So, for example, I might go a bit further and point out that it is because of the oil company conspiracy that we see not only the artificial rise in the price of oil but also that lobbyists represent the entire oil industry, not individual oil companies, in the halls of Congress. Moreover, it explains why a few very influential congressmen accept large political donations from the oil industry and even why it is that we see so few independent gas stations today—gas stations not owned by the major oil companies. Now, a whole series of rather interesting facts are explained by a single conspiracy. Yet in bringing in these additional facts, I am only showing that my theory can be extended to explain a lot. I have yet to provide any evidence that it is true. Though it no doubt sounds intriguing (who among us does not enjoy a good conspiracy?), my theory has yet to be supported by a single independent test.

No doubt there are conspiracies and conspirators, but their existence cannot be proven simply by spinning stories that would, if true, account for a myriad of interesting facts. One antidote to fallacious conspiracy theories involves considering the possibility of a discrete explanation for each of the facts the theory purportedly explains. It may be, for example, that the reason that congressmen accept large donations from the oil industry has little to do with the actual explanation for the demise of many independent gas stations.

In addition to conspiracy theories, we should be wary of any attempt to vindicate an explanation by treating known facts as though they were predictive consequences of the explanation. If I know X, I cannot "predict" X as a means of defending a particular explanation for X. One evening not too long ago, I passed a person I had never seen before just prior to entering my unlocked office to pick up some tests that needed to be graded. But the tests were missing! My initial hunch was that the stranger took the tests from my office. Now, it may be that my hunch is right. But suppose someone were to doubt the correctness of my explanation. I do not provide independent evidence for my explanation by again citing the facts that have prompted my explanation—namely, that I observed the stranger near my office, that the office was unlocked, and that the papers were missing.

Claims of extraordinary abilities and events are often made in such a way that they are unfalsifiable. An astrologer claims to be able to tell us something of what awaits us in the future based on our astrological chart. "Expect to move to the east coast within the next six months," says our astrologer. "However, always remember, the stars impel, they don't compel." Thus, the prediction is vindicated if we move east but also if we do not, for we can always choose to change the possible future laid out in our chart. Equally unfalsifiable, though for a different reason, would be this prediction: "You'll be making a significant trip within the next six months." No doubt this is right. I, for one, plan on making an important trip to the bank to deposit a large sum of money to cover my overdraft, just as soon as I receive my paycheck. Here our astrologer has guaranteed success not by explaining in advance a possible failed prediction, but by making a prediction that is so vague that it will "fit" an enormous variety of likely events.

Illicit ad hoc rescues.   Explanations and claimed extraordinary abilities need not be dismissed simply because, in a given test, they appear to be false. As we said in Chapter 2, it is always worthwhile to consider various auxiliary assumptions made in conjunction with a test. It may be that failure is due to a questionable assumption we have made in setting up the experiment. In the event that we fail to get the result we expected, we might want to modify our test and try again. But this sort of holding maneuver can only take us so far. If numerous modifications yield no different results, there is a point at which we must admit that our initial expectations were wrong. To persist in defending our expectations after it is clear they are probably wrong is to engage in what is called an illicit *ad hoc rescue.*

Suppose someone has advanced an explanation, but subsequent tests fail to confirm it. The effect of an ad hoc rescue is to suggest a new explanation for the failure to confirm the original explanation. Nothing is wrong with such a maneuver provided the new, ad hoc explanation can itself be independently tested. In fact, such maneuvers are part and parcel of the way in which science is done. Such a move is illicit, however, if it is advanced only to "save" the original explanation by proposing something that, if true, would account for the failure to confirm the original explanation.

The discovery of the planet Neptune provides a good example of the sort of legitimate ad hoc rescue that occurs in scientific research. In the early 1800s, six of the seven known planets in our solar system seemed to obey laws set forth by Kepler and Newton. But the outermost planet, Uranus, moved on a course considerably different from that predicted by these laws. Now, one possibility was that the laws in question were a special case, only capable of explaining the motions of some of the planets. Another possibility, however, suggested a way for the laws in question to retain their generality. In the mid-1800s, astronomers speculated that the peculiar movement of Uranus could be explained in a way consistent with Newton and Kepler if another planet were to exist out beyond the orbit of Uranus. (The gravitational attraction of the newly postulated planet would account for the problems.) Now, at this point in the story, we must regard the proposed new planet as part of an ad hoc rescue; If there is such a planet, the laws in question retain their generality. Fortunately, astronomers were able to predict just where the new planet should be in order to exert the postulated gravitational influence on Uranus, and shortly thereafter Neptune was discovered precisely where predicted. The ad hoc rescue thus turned out to be justified.

By way of contrast, consider the following. Imagine that a psychic has agreed to be tested and further agrees that he or she can perform under the experimental conditions we have set up. Unfortunately, the psychic fails. Nevertheless, claims our psychic, this does not show that he or she cannot do the things in question. For psychic abilities are subject to something called the "shyness effect": Psychic abilities ebb and flow and frequently seem to ebb just when we want them to flow. It is almost, adds our psychic, as though they don't want to be tested. It would seem that the psychic's appeal to the shyness effect is not calculated to help us rethink our experiment, particularly if there is no independent way of testing for its presence or absence. Rather, it is nothing more than an attempt to make sure that, no matter how carefully we design our experimental test, no conceivable result need be taken as repudiating the psychic's claimed ability. By contrast with the legitimate ad hoc rescue that ended in the discovery of Neptune, our psychic's maneuver seems clearly to constitute an illicit ad hoc rescue. It would appear to be untestable, and its only redeeming feature is that, if true, it would "save" our psychic in the face of his or her failure to perform under controlled conditions.

Science and Pseudoscience

All of the ways we have considered in which scientific inquiry can go astray suggest something of a problem. How do we determine whether a result, advanced in the name of science, is genuine or bogus? Our discussion of fallacious uses of the methods of science suggests one crucial difference between genuine science on the one hand, and pseudoscience—fake science—on the other: Genuine science involves the rigorous testing of new ideas, employing the methods introduced in Chapters 2 through 4; pseudoscientific ideas will frequently be backed by evidence that is the product of one or more of the fallacies discussed in this chapter. Though adherence to the methods of science is at the heart of the distinction between genuine science and pseudoscience, there are a number of other important differences between the two, as well as number of mistaken ideas about what the distinction involves.

Science cannot be distinguished from pseudoscience on the basis of the quality of the results each produces.   In science, at any rate, ideas earn their respectability not because they are right, but because they have been tested in the right sort of way. Many of the examples we have considered here and in preceding chapters serve to confirm this. At one point in the history of Western thought, the best-informed scientific view was that the earth is at the center of the universe. Though this view was ultimately shown to be wrong, it nonetheless constituted the best science of the time. Though Ptolemy and his followers were mistaken, their view of the cosmos provided a coherent, testable explanation for a wide variety of phenomena. Our discussion earlier in this chapter of the luminiferous ether provides another striking example of genuine, though ultimately mistaken, science.

The distinction between science and pseudoscience cannot be drawn along lines of scientific discipline.   We cannot say, for example, that astronomy is a science whereas astrology is not, that psychology is but psychic research isn't. This is not to say that astronomy or psychology does not deserve to be called a science. But the notion of a science, or scientific discipline, is much too broad for our purposes. My dictionary defines astronomy as "the science which treats of the heavenly bodies—stars, planets, satellites and comets," and I suppose this is as good a definition as any other. But within this broad discipline, we sometimes do encounter instances of pseudoscience as well as of genuine science.

For example, in the 1950s, a self-proclaimed astronomer and archeologist, Immanuel Velikovsky, hypothesized that the planet Venus was created out of an enormous volcanic eruption on Jupiter. Velikovsky speculated that as the newly formed planet hurled toward the sun, it passed by the earth, causing several cataclysmic events, and eventually settled down to become the second planet in our solar system. Yet careful examination of Velikovsky's work has shown that this sort of cosmic Ping-Pong is quite impossible and that Velikovsky either ignored or was unaware of certain physical constraints that his hypothesis violated. One of Velilovsky's most glaring mistakes involves a well-known law of motion: If one body exerts a force on a second body, then the second exerts a force that is equal in strength and opposite in direction. An explosion of sufficient magnitude to allow an object the size of Venus to overcome the gravitational attraction of Jupiter would simultaneously send Jupiter off in the opposite direction, despite Jupiter's great mass. Yet in Velikovsky's theory, the orbit of Jupiter remains unaffected by this most cataclysmic of events. Here, then, we have an example of pseudoscience, yet one that we can certainly classify under the broad heading of astronomy.

Similarly, early in this century, British psychologist Sir Cyril Burt claimed to have decisive evidence that heredity, not environment, plays the dominant role in determining intelligence. Yet as it turned out, much of Burt's work was based on fictional or distorted data. Burt apparently invented experimental subjects and altered test results to conform to his expectations in the process of trying to make his findings appear to be scientific.

The distinction between science and pseudoscience has nothing to do with the distinction between "hard" and "soft" sciences. The sciences that study human behavior—sociology, anthropology, psychology, political science, to name a few—are sometimes characterized as "soft," as opposed to the "hard" physical and biological sciences. Although the soft and hard sciences differ in a number of respects, none of the differences is sufficient to support the complaint, occasionally leveled against the soft disciplines, that they are pseudosciences. The hard sciences, in their attempts at describing and understanding nature, do not have to deal with the complexities posed by the human ability to choose what to do. It is sometimes said that only the hard sciences are "exact," and this is generally taken to mean that predictions about human behavior cannot hope to be as precise as, say, predictions about what will happen to a gas under a specific set of conditions. Moreover, it is difficult to think of a single "soft" scientific theory that is as broad in scope as the theories of modern physics and chemistry. The law of gravity describes the behavior of all gravitating objects; it is hard to imagine a similar law describing a single aspect of the behavior of people, societies, economic systems, or political institutions.

Yet despite their obvious differences, the hard and soft sciences are all properly called sciences. All aim at explaining phenomena of the natural world, be it the behavior of matter or the behavior of human beings. And both hard and soft sciences adhere to the methods we have discussed in Chapters 2 through 4 in advancing and testing their "hows" and "whys." Many philosophers argue that the social sciences will never produce the kinds of grand, unifying theories characteristic of the physical and biological sciences; it may be that the "soft" sciences will have to be satisfied with discrete bits of explanatory material, each of which is suited to a limited aspect of human behavior. But insofar as research in the social and behavioral sciences conforms to the more general methods of good scientific research, we have no reason to doubt their qualifications as disciplines capable of delivering genuine scientific results.

Genuine science tends to be self-correcting; pseudoscience is not. We have examined a number of instances in which the results of scientific inquiry have been overturned.; in most cases, mistaken ideas have been rejected on the basis of further scientific inquiry. It is estimated that there are currently about 40,000 active scientific journals worldwide. The function of such a journal is to report new findings and results and, equally important, to provide a forum for the critics of current research. Interestingly enough, most criticism of potentially pseudoscientific research comes from within mainstream science as well. Recent criticism of the work of the special creationists, for example, has been leveled by mainstream anthropologists, zoologists, biologists, and evolutionary theorists. Although there are a few journals devoted to creationist science, it is rare to find a single article by a noted creationist critical of the work of other creationists.

As a scientific discipline develops, it will gradually produce a maturing body of explanatory or theoretical findings; pseudoscience produces very little theory.   One major aim of science, as we discussed in Chapter 1, is to "make sense" of nature by providing better and better and, often, more and more encompassing bodies of explanatory material. Think, for example, of all that is known about the mechanisms involved in the transmission of genetic information from one generation to the next, by contrast with what was known 150 years ago when the science of genetics was born. Gregor Mendel, the first great figure in the field of genetic research, began by speculating about "genetic factors" that might be responsible for observable characteristics in some simple varieties of plants. Today, modern geneticists speak of the subtle and complex methods by which DNA is transmitted in any organism.

By contrast, pseudoscientific research almost always produces spectacular claims for extraordinary abilities and events, but little else. Moreover, the nature of the claims produced varies little over time. As it turns out, ESP research began only a little later than did genetic research. Yet today we find little more than an enormous body of controversial evidence that a few people have psychic ability and almost no theoretical understanding of how ESP might work. In many pseudoscientific endeavors, what little explanatory material emerges is likely to be based on vague analogies and similarities drawn from some well-understood area of science. Thus, for example, a book on ESP published in the 1930s was entitled *ESP: Mental Radio*. An interesting idea, but hardly a reliable explanation.

The findings, theoretical and otherwise, of genuine science are always open to revision; rarely do pseudoscientific claims change much over time.   It is hard to imagine a thriving scientific discipline today in which much of what was believed 100 or even 50 years ago has not been supplanted by a more accurate picture of things. Fifty years ago, particle physics provide us with a picture of the world in which the most fundamental particles were the electron, proton, and neutron. A few stray experimental results conflicted with this picture, but few physicists questioned its rough fit with reality. Today, physics provides a more comprehensive picture in which protons and neutrons are composites built out of even more fundamental particles, quarks. The landscape of particle physics has change dramatically in a brief period of time.

By way of contrast, it is interesting to look at the work of modern astrologers. If you were to have a competent astrologer draw a detailed horoscope, his or her work would be based on classic astrological texts written nearly 2000 years ago. Pseudoscientists often claim the long history of their ideas as evidence for their correctness. Thus, an astrologer might boast that his or her techniques are derived from the discoveries of ancient Babylonian and Egyptian astronomers. But from a scientific point of view, any idea that undergoes little or no revision over such a long period of time is probably not the product of careful scientific investigation.

Genuine science embraces skepticism; pseudoscience tends to view skepticism as a sign of narrow-mindedness. The first reaction of a competent scientist, when faced with something new and unusual, is to try to explain the phenomenon by fitting it into what is already known. Many people who engage in pseudoscience see this as the worst sort of skepticism; the fact that one's initial reaction is to try to rob something of its mystery is taken as a sign that one is unwilling to entertain new ideas. It is perhaps this attitude toward scientific skepticism more than anything else that contributes to the tendency in pseudoscience to accept claims in the absence of solid scientific evidence.

The question of whether a piece of "scientific" research is genuine or bogus is not always easy to answer. Though the points of contrast we have highlighted here can provide us with some initial sense of when we are in the presence of pseudoscience, we should not wield them dogmatically. If people purport to have "scientific evidence" for something, we should not dismiss their work simply because, for example, they refuse to countenance serious criticism, complain that their critics lack an open mind, or proclaim the longevity of their ideas. However, such moves should be taken as a sign that something may be seriously amiss. The fundamental difference between genuine and bogus science is really a difference in method. The results of genuine scientific inquiry are the product of open, honest applications of the methods we have discussed in previous chapters. Pseudoscientific results, by contrast, are produced with little regard for these methods.

A person claims to have "scientific evidence" for X. Are we confronted with genuine science or pseudoscience? To answer this question, there is no substitute for taking a careful, critical look at the methods employed in establishing X.

The Limits of Scientific Explanation

In Chapter 1, we said that one major goal of science is to further our understanding of how and why things happen as they do. In Chapters 2 through 5, we have taken a close look at the method by which science attempts to accomplish this goal and at some of the ways in which the methods of science can be abused. One further issue, however, deserves some brief discussion before we conclude: Are there "hows" and "whys" that science cannot help us to answer? Are there things, that is, that science is powerless to explain?

With respect to questions about processes occurring in the natural world, it is hard to imagine a limit to the potential of science to explain. This does not mean that science, given enough time and effort, will provide us with an understanding of all natural processes. What it does mean is that there appears to be no limit to the questions—questions about the natural world—that science, properly carried out, cannot profitably address. And if it turns out that there are such limits, we will discover them only by approaching them scientifically and discovering just how far this approach can carry us.

But there other "hows" and other "whys"—"hows" and "whys" that take us beyond the interests normally associated with scientific inquiry. These are the great questions of metaphysics, questions that have vexed philosophers and ordinary people alike for as long as people have thought. They are questions you have probably wondered about in some idle moment: Why is there anything at all, rather than nothing? Is there some benevolent, creative force responsible for the natural world? Is there, in other words, a God? Why are we here? Do our lives have some ultimate meaning, some cosmic purpose?

Deep metaphysical questions like these, I suspect, will not be settled by scientific inquiry. This is not to suggest that science is somehow deficient. The methods of science are not designed to answer questions of this sort. Science aims to explain processes occurring within the natural world; these deep metaphysical questions raise issues about the nature of the natural world itself. They are not concerned with mechanisms, causes, laws, the very stuff of scientific explanation. They involve, rather, an attempt to understand the purposes behind the sum total of the natural world. If scientific questions are, by definition, questions about how and why things happen in the natural world, then metaphysical question are, by definition, not scientific questions. Even if science were somehow, someday to provide us with an utterly complete explanatory picture of all processes in nature—a theory of everything—science would still leave our deep metaphysical questions untouched. Why this particular set of explanations and not another? What is their cosmic significance? Their purpose? Who is their author?

Not long before his death, Sir Peter Medawar, Nobel laureate in medicine, made the following observation:

> Catastrophe apart, I believe it to be science's greatest glory that there is no limit upon the power of science to answer questions of the kind science *can* answer.[5]

Metaphysical questions aside, there would seem to be no limit to the ability of science to explain as long as we restrict science to the kind of question, as Medawar says, science can answer.

Summary

Here is a brief summary of the fallacies we have discussed and of the telltale signs of a pseudoscience.

Fallacies in Scientific Reasoning

Fallacies Involving Initial Observations

Anecdotal evidence: basing a general claim on a few anecdotal reports.

Omitting facts: creating an air of mystery by leaving out facts that might account for the mystery.

Distorting the facts: altering the facts to create the impression that something is mysterious

Fallacies Involving Rival Explanations

Fallacious argument by elimination: arguing for a given explanation by attempting to show that rival explanations are wrong.

Fallacious inference to a causal link: inferring a causal link on the basis of a correlation, concomitant variation, or the fact that the suspected cause occurred before its effect. Possible rival explanations are coincidence, fudging of data, and third factors.

Fallacies in Proposing and Testing Explanations

Exploiting analogies and similarities: treating explanations for well-understood phenomena as though they were evidence for a similar explanation for something not so well understood.

Proposing unfalsifiable claims: (1) advancing a claim, explanatory or otherwise, that is consistent with everything that could happen; (2) working with predictions that cannot be falsified; (3) explaining away all conceivable experimental results that might suggest that a claim is false; or (4) treating initiating facts as confirming facts.

Illicit ad hoc rescues: advancing auxiliary assumptions that cannot be independently verified as a means of saving an explanation or extraordinary claim.

The Telltale Signs of Pseudoscience

1. Pseudoscientific claims often involve fallacious scientific reasoning of the sort exemplified by the preceding fallacies.
2. Pseudoscience can occur within the bounds of legitimate scientific disciplines.
3. Pseudoscience tends not to be self-correcting.
4. Pseudoscience produces very little explanatory theory.
5. Rarely do pseudoscientific claims change much over time.
6. Pseudoscientists tend to view skepticism as a sign of narrow-mindedness.

Exercises

Many of the following passages involve one or more of the fallacies we have discussed. Comment on any fallacies you find; name them, and explain in more detail how the passage involves the fallacy or fallacies you have uncovered. When appropriate, speculate about rival explanations that are overlooked. Look for examples of the other characteristic features of pseudoscience, and comment on any you find.

Problems you will encounter in some of the passages will be difficult to classify; in thinking about mistakes they may involve, you will need to rely on your by now well-developed sense of what good scientific research involves. In other words, you may need to apply some of the ideas presented in Chapters 2 through 4.

(Note: A solution to Exercise 1 is provided on page 118.)

1. A remarkable fact is that many of the great scientists and mathematicians in history have had a deep interest in music. Einstein, for example, was a devoted amateur violinist, and Newton is said to have been fascinated by the mathematical structure of musical compositions. If you want your child to pursue a career in science, you would be well advised to do everything you can to develop his or her interest in music.

2. The following is excerpted from a recent article in the *Weekly World News* entitled "First Photo of a Human Soul":

   > What was expected to be a routine heart surgery wound up making religious and medical history when a photographer snapped a picture of the patient's body a split second after she died. The dramatic photo clearly shows a glowing angelic spirit rising up off the operating table as the line of Karin Fisher's heart monitor went flat at the moment of death. And while nobody in the operating theater actually saw the strange entity as it left the 32-year-old patient's body, scholars, clergymen and the Vatican itself are hailing the photo as the most dramatic proof of life after death ever.
   >
   > "This is it. This is the proof that true believers the world over have been waiting for," Dr. Martin Muller, who has conducted an extensive study of the picture, told reporters.
   >
   > Oddly enough, not one of the 12 doctors, nurses and technicians in the operating room saw the glowing spirit leave the woman's body, apparently because it wasn't visible to the naked eye.
   >
   > But as a matter of routine the procedure was photographed by the hospital's director of education, Peter Valentin, who found a single black and white picture of the spirit among 72 prints that were made.
   >
   > "The photo has been the focus of intense study and debate for several weeks now and the consensus of both scholars and clergymen is that it is indeed authentic," said Dr. Muller.
   >
   > "That's not to say that there aren't any skeptics because there are," he continued.
   >
   > "The problem with their position is that they can offer no alternative explanations for the flowing image that turned up on the picture. In fact, there are no alternative explanations. You either accept the image in faith, as I do, or you reject it. There is no in-between."[6]

3. Acupuncture has been practiced in Asia for nearly 3000 years. It is based on the belief that the mind and body are a continuum, a self-contained bioelectric system through which runs a river of energy called *qi* or *ch'i*. Two opposite currents flow in this river,

yin (night, dark, cold, female) and *yang* (day, light, hot, male), and well-being requires that they be balanced. Illness and pain occur when they are not, when metabolic waste and energy back up at the site of an injury.

By using hair-thin needles, a burning herb called moxa that heats the inserted needle, thereby intensifying its stimulation, and, on very rare occasions, electrodes, acupuncturists are able to regulate the flow of the *qi* through 12 channels called meridians. To do so, they place needles at any one or several of the 2000 named points that correspond to the body's muscles, organs, and systems.

4. Graphologists claim to be able to tell a great deal about people from their handwriting. The following is from a report prepared for the author by a professional graphologist:

> You are a person who is alive to the world about you, and you react quickly and in a friendly way to those who show you a friendly interest. You are easily influenced by life's many joys and sorrows, and your first response to any situation in life, pleasant or unpleasant, will be an emotionally responsive one. Even though you are strongly influenced by the way you feel, you will not go to extremes and allow your emotions to rule your life by controlling you entirely.

5. You have probably heard about backmasking—inserting subliminal messages in recordings of popular music in reverse. In fact, some people claim that if you play such recordings backward, you can actually hear the message. But have you ever wondered how the mind deciphers the message, given that it hears it backward? Well, the answer is quite simple. We do not hear individual words when we listen to speech or lyrics. Instead, we hear whole sentences constructed, like a chain of linked metal loops, of the individual words. The whole sentences can be processed by the brain either forward or backward, much as a linked chain can be dragged back and forth.

6. Though most reports of UFOs can be explained in perfectly ordinary ways—sightings of weather balloons, blimps, the moon, and so on—there remains a small residue of cases that have no known explanation. These sightings are typically by reliable people and are often reported by a number of observers. Thus, we can rule out the possibility of a hoax of some sort. It seems clear, then, that we have evidence that earth has been visited by beings from another planet or star system.

7. The following passage is from an article in *Impact*, a publication of the Institute for Creation Research, entitled "Modern Scientific Discovery Verifies the Scriptures":

> If there is a second law of thermodynamics, there must be a first law, of course. Indeed there is, and this natural law confirms another scientifically testable statement found in the Bible. The First Law of Thermodynamics states that the total quantity of energy and matter in the universe is a constant. One form of energy may be converted into another, energy may be converted into matter, and matter may be converted into energy, but the total quantity always remains the same. The First Law of Thermodynamics, the most firmly established law in natural science, confirms the Biblical statement concerning a finished creation, as found in Genesis 2:1.2: "Thus the heavens and the earth were finished, and all the host of

them. And on the seventh day God ended His work which He had made; and He rested on the seventh day from all His work which He had made."

If it could be shown that somewhere in this universe matter or energy was coming into being from nothing, then this Biblical statement of a finished creation would be falsified. The opposite is true. It has been precisely verified. Once again, a Biblical statement has withstood scientific test.

8. Is it just a coincidence that there are so many parallels between the lives of two famous people who lived at different times? Perhaps. But perhaps not. It may be that we have lived past lives and that certain of our traits persist from lifetime to lifetime. You are no doubt aware of some of the eerie similarities between John F. Kennedy and Abraham Lincoln. This is only the tip of the iceberg. Consider the strange parallels between the lives of George Washington and Dwight Eisenhower:

   a. Both came to prominence as victorious generals.
   b. Both served two full terms as president.
   c. Both gave famous farewell speeches warning the United States against foolish military policies.
   d. Both were replaced as president by Harvard graduates named John, from wealthy, prominent Massachusetts families.
   e. *Eisenhower* and *Washington* have ten letters each.
   f. *Dwight* and *George* have six letters each.
   g. Neither belonged to a political party before seeking the presidency.

9. "What goes around comes around." In this simple statement lies one of the most profound truths about human destiny, sometimes called the Law of Karma. Even the Bible recognizes this most fundamental of truths: "As ye sow, so shall ye reap." You may think there are bound to be exceptions to this cosmic law of justice. After all, people do not always suffer the consequences of the bad things they do, nor are they consistently rewarded for the good. But have faith. The results of our actions may not catch up with us in this life, but there are other lives. What we sow in this existence, we may reap in another incarnation.

10. A recent study of 50 of America's most profitable companies revealed some interesting facts. Many of the companies have resisted the temptation to expand into new and unfamiliar industries. Or, as Robert W. Johnson, former chairman of Johnson and Johnson, put it, "Never acquire a business you don't know how to run." It seems clear that the odds increase that a large company will remain profitable over the long haul if it sticks to doing business in areas with which it is familiar.

11. Some psychics claim to be able to help police with cases, usually those involving missing persons or unsolved murders. These "psychic detectives" claim that they "work with" police departments as "consultants" on many of their unsolved cases. Typically, a psychic will go to the scene of a crime or the place where a person was last seen before disappearing and, using ESP, will "see" important facts pertaining to the case.

In fact, there are very few instances in which the police initiate a request for help from a psychic. In most cases, the parents or relatives of a missing or dead person contact a psychic, pay for the person's help, and then offer the findings to the local police department.

12. A recent study suggests that near-death experiences may have a physiological or psychological explanation. In the study, the medical records of 100 patients who would have died without medical intervention were compared with those of another 100 patients who were not in danger of dying but who thought they were. The researchers discovered that about the same number of subjects in each group—32 in the first group and 35 in the second—reported having near-death experiences.

I think we must take the results of this study with a grain of salt. It may be that the people who mistakenly believed they were near death somehow inadvertently triggered the psycho/physiological mechanism by which the soul leaves the body. Thus, though they mistakenly believed they were near death, their near-death experiences were nonetheless genuine.

Exercises 13–15 are all taken from Bio-Rhythm: A Personal Science.[7] *Biorhythm is the theory that from birth to death each of us is influenced by three internal cycles—the physical, the emotional, and the intellectual.*

13. On the evening of November 11, 1960, a retired Swiss importer named George Thommen was interviewed on the "Long John Nebel Show," a radio talkathon based in New York City. What Thommen had to say sounded surprising to most people and incredible to some. However, the strangest thing Thommen said was in the form of a warning. He cautioned that Clark Gable, who was then in the hospital recovering from a heart attack suffered six days before while filming *The Misfits* with Marilyn Monroe, would have to be very careful on November 16. On that date, explained Thommen, Gable's "physical rhythm" would be "critical." As a result, his condition would be unstable, putting him in danger of a relapse.

Few listeners took Thommen's warning seriously. Gable and his doctors were probably unaware of it. On Wednesday, November 16, 1960, Clark Gable suffered an unexpected second heart attack and died. His doctor later admitted that his life might have been saved if the needed medical equipment had been in place beside his bed when he was stricken a second time.

14. Actually, the theory of biorhythm is little more than an extension and generalization of the enormous amount of research that scientists have already done on the many biological rhythms and cycles of life. From the migration of swallows and the feeding patterns of oysters to the levels of hormones in human blood and the patterns of sleep, life can be defined as regulated time. Countless rhythms, most of them fairly predictable, can be found in even the simplest of our bodily functions. Even the smallest component of our bodies, the cell, follows several clearly defined cycles as it creates and uses up energy.

15. There is nothing in biorhythm theory that contradicts scientific knowledge. . . . But until we can perform strictly controlled studies of how and why biorhythm works, and until many other researchers have been able to replicate these studies, we will have to base

the case for biorhythm on purely empirical research. . . . Ultimately, however, the most convincing studies of biorhythm are those you can do yourself. By working out your own biorhythm chart and biorhythm profiles for particular days, and then comparing them with your experiences of up and down days, of illness and health, of success and failure, you will be able to judge for yourself.

16. Sociobiology is the theory that the major component of social behavior is biological adaptation. In the view of many sociobiologists, the structure of human and animal societies is determined, in large measure, by the innate biological impulse to increase that species' chances of survival. One large difficulty faced by the sociobiologist is the existence of social arrangements that appear to be of little adaptive value, yet appear to occur in all human cultures. Why, for example, is there a significant number of homosexuals in all cultures, given that procreation is necessary for survival? One sociobiologist has suggested that in primitive societies homosexuals, because they were free of parental obligations, could help their close relatives with unrivaled efficiency. If they succeeded, their relatives would produce more children, thus passing on their genes to the next generation. Similarly, religions may have developed in many human cultures as a means of giving members of the culture a driving purpose that would motivate a desire to survive and to pass wisdom to future generations.

17. For years, stories have been circulating about an internal combustion engine, invented sometime in the 1950s, that burns a simple combination of hydrogen and oxygen instead of gasoline. This "water engine," as it is sometimes called, could revolutionize the world economy by freeing us of our dependence on fossil fuels and making transportation virtually free to everyone. But don't hold your breath. The major players in the global economy are a tight confederation of industries and countries involved in the manufacture, maintenance, and fueling of automobiles. So enormous is the global monetary investment in the status quo that it is virtually impossible that the water engine will ever see the light of day. The major oil and automotive companies have seen to it that all patents pertaining to this revolutionary new invention are under their control, and they have orchestrated the suppression of all information about this incredible new invention that would, if marketed, cost them billions of dollars. Ask any representative of the oil or automotive industry—or any government official, for that matter—about the water engine and I predict this is just what you will hear: either "No comment" or "There's simply no such thing."

18. You don't think there is anything to astrology? Well, consider this. Last week, I was at a meeting of the local chapter of the American Philosophical Association. There were only about 50 philosophers at the meeting, yet three were born on the same day of the year, and two other pairs of philosophers also shared birthdays!

19. The following newspaper article appeared under the heading "Ex-OSU Professor Theorizes About Alien Beings":

> Aliens from distant worlds may be watching earth and making unofficial contact with selected humans, says a recently retired scientist at Oregon State University. His theory is that advanced and benevolent space beings may have adopted an

embargo on official contact with earthlings, wishing to avoid the chaos that could sweep the planet if their presence were suddenly revealed.

Instead, they have adopted a "leaky embargo" policy that allows contact only with citizens whose stories are unlikely to be credible to scientists and the government, said the scientist, James W. Deardorff, 58, professor emeritus of atmospheric sciences.

"They just want to let those know who are prepared to accept it in their minds that there are other beings," Deardorff said. "They may want to slowly prepare us for the shock that could come later when they reveal themselves. . . ."

Deardorff is prepared to accept many ideas looked upon skeptically by other scientists, including telepathy and the possibility of time travel and physical dimensions other than space and time.

His open-mindedness has made it more difficult to operate in the scientific mainstream, where scientific committees have been formed to debunk theories about UFO's and psychic phenomena.

"There's a lot of polarization going on now," he said, adding that he has had trouble getting some papers on extraterrestrials published in scientific journals. "There's a lot less middle ground than there used to be," he said. "It's no accident that I'm getting more active in this area now after retirement."[8]

20. I have a new theory about that most mysterious of forces, gravity. Though physicists can describe the laws that gravity follows, they have failed entirely to explain the mechanism by which gravity works. I think I have the answer. Every massive object in the universe generates invisible, springlike tendrils in the direction of every other object in its immediate vicinity. When these tendrils connect, they function like a coiled spring, with the tension varying in direct proportion to the product of the masses of the objects they connect and in inverse proportion to the square of the distance between the objects. I call these tendrils "virtual springs." Thus, virtual springs grow in strength as objects are closer together and weaken as objects recede from one another. That I am onto something remarkable is suggested by the following. If my virtual spring theory is right, objects of differing masses should all accelerate toward another massive object, say, the surface of the earth, and, moreover, should do so at roughly the same rate. By careful experimentation I have established the truth of both these predictions. Massive objects all tend to fall toward the earth and tend to do so at precisely the same rate of acceleration, irrespective of differences in mass!

21. Telekinesis is the ability to bring about physical changes by purely mental processes. Is telekinesis for real? Consider the following experiment. A computer is programmed to generate numbers at random. When an odd number is generated, the computer prints out "odd"; when an even number is generated, it prints out "even." An experimenter instructs the computer to proceed, one number at a time. Prior to the generation of each number, an experimental subject is instructed to think "odd" or "even" and then to mark down his or her choice on a tally sheet. The experimenter then instructs the computer to generate a number, and the result is tallied against the choice of the experimental subject. Several hundred trials are run in this way. Under these experimental conditions, it is predicted that subjects with telekinetic ability will score much higher

than chance would predict—that is, the computer and the experimental subject will agree more than 50% of the time.

22. From a newspaper article:

> A Harvard team that discovered an apparent link between coffee and cancer of the pancreas has published new research that disputes its own earlier finding.
>
> "Standing alone, it's very difficult to know what conclusions to draw from this," said Dr. Brian MacMahon of the Harvard School of Public Health.
>
> Five years ago, MacMahon's team published a study concluding that people who drink a cup or two of coffee a day are nearly twice as likely as non-drinkers to get pancreatic cancer. Methods used to reach that conclusion were criticized by some and later follow-ups by other groups did not find a strong association between coffee and cancer.
>
> The team's latest study, published as a letter in Thursday's *New England Journal of Medicine*, found no increased cancer risk for people who drink less than five cups a day.
>
> For those who consumed more than that, the results were less clear. Men who drank five or more cups a day had nearly $2\frac{1}{2}$ times the usual risk for pancreatic cancer, but there was no statistically significant increase in risk among women.
>
> MacMahon noted that the latest research turned up no evidence of a gradual increase in risk as consumption rose. Such a trend would be expected if coffee truly caused cancer.
>
> "I think the association is almost certainly not as strong as we originally found it," said MacMahon. "But whether there is an association at all is still an open question. If I had to come down one way or the other, I would say probably there is not, but I don't think it's a situation where one should come down hard one way or the other."

23. From a flyer advertising a chiropractic clinic:

> Ronald Pero, Ph.D., researched the immune system at the University of Lund Medical School, Lund, Sweden, and the Preventative Medical Institute, New York City. He measured both immune resistance to disease and the ability to repair genetic damage.
>
> In a news report about his study in *East/West Journal*, November 1989, chiropractic patients were compared to two groups: normal, healthy people and cancer patients. The chiropractic patients were all in long-term care on a wellness basis. Their immune function was measured to be two times stronger than the healthy people, and four times stronger than the sick! And this increase occurred regardless of age. With ongoing chiropractic care, the immune system does not deteriorate, as in other groups.

24. From an ad for past life drawings—drawings by a psychic of the way we looked in our past lives:

> Since I've been doing Past Life Drawings and Readings for people, I'm often amazed at how relevant the information is in their present lives. Even though we

may have had thousands of incarnations, I've found that there are usually three main past lives which are influencing our present lives the most.

One woman that I did drawings for had a past life in India as a young male who rode and trained elephants to lift logs and move stones to build a temple. Years later when the temple was completed, the man decided to spend the rest of his life meditating in the temple. The woman revealed that she had been doing Eastern meditation for many years and she also had a large ceramic elephant lamp, elephant bookends and other elephant figurines all around the house.

One man had an unpleasant life on a ship which ended when he was tied and thrown overboard into the ocean and drowned. The man had always been afraid of water in this life and never learned to swim. I worked with this man to bring the drowning experience into the present time and helped him to release the emotions and fear connected with it. A month later he was swimming and inner-tubing in Timothy Lake with his wife and sons.

25. Many strange and wonderful things are attributed to the mysterious power of the pyramid. For example, you can increase the life of a razor blade by keeping it stored inside a simple plastic pyramid. If you don't believe me, try this simple experiment. After you use your razor, remove the blade, wash it in warm water, and then dry the blade off. Finally, place it inside or under a small pyramid-shaped container. I think you will be surprised at how long the blade retains its sharpness.

26. If you are wondering how pyramids manage to accomplish this marvelous feat, consider the following explanation by G. Patrick Flannigen, self-proclaimed pyramid power expert: The shape of the pyramid acts as a sort of lens or focus for the transmission of biocosmic energy.

27. I've had it with my local supermarket. Every time I shop there, it seems they're out of something I need. Only yesterday I stopped to pick up a cantaloupe on my way home and, wouldn't you know, they were out. And just last week they were out of the ice cream they had on sale. I'm going to start shopping somewhere where they do a better job of managing their inventory.

28. A recent study has shown that, on average, a graduate of an Ivy League college will make more money over the course of his or her career than a graduate of any other college. Moreover, a graduate of an East Coast college will make more than a graduate of a midwestern, southern, or western college. It seems clear that if you want to make it financially, you ought to try to get into an Ivy League school and, if you can't get in, at least go to college on the East Coast.

29. The following newspaper story appeared under the headline, "Gyroscope Test Possibly Defies Gravity":

> Japanese scientists have reported that small gyroscopes lose weight when spun under certain conditions, apparently in defiance of gravity. If proved correct, the finding would mark a stunning scientific advance, but experts said they doubted that it would survive intense scrutiny.

A systematic way to negate gravitation, the attraction between all masses and particles of matter in the universe, has eluded scientists since the principles of the force were first elucidated by Isaac Newton in the 17th century.

The anti-gravity work is reported in the Dec. 18, 1989, issue of *Physical Review Letters*, which is regarded by experts as one of the world's leading journals of physics and allied fields. Its articles are rigorously reviewed by other scientists before being accepted for publication, and it rejects far more than it accepts.

Experts who have seen the report said that it seemed to be based on sound research and appeared to have no obvious sources of experimental error, but they cautioned that other seemingly reliable reports have collapsed under close examination.

The work was performed by Hideo Hayasaka and Sakae Takeuchi of the engineering faculty at Tohoku University in Sendai, Japan.

Unlike the exaggerated claims made for low-temperature or "cold" nuclear fusion this year, the current results are presented with scientific understatement. The authors do not claim to have defied gravity, but simply say their results "cannot be explained by the usual theories."

"It's an astounding claim," said Robert L. Park, a professor of physics at the University of Maryland who is director of the Washington office of the American Physical Society, which publishes *Physical Review Letters*. "It would be revolutionary if true. But it's almost certainly wrong. Almost all extraordinary claims are wrong."

The experiment looked at weight changes in spinning gyroscopes whose rotors weighed 140 and 176 grams, or 5 and 6.3 ounces. When the gyroscopes were spun clockwise, as viewed from above, the researchers found no change in their weight. But when spun counterclockwise, they appeared to lose weight.[9]

30. It seems that children who spend more time watching popular programs on commercial television tend to be lower achievers in school. Several studies have established that performance on standardized tests varies in inverse proportion to the amount of television a child under the age of 12 watches. The more television of this sort a child watches, the lower his or her scores are likely to be.

31. Nostradamus, a 16-century French physician, is said to have predicted with great accuracy things that occurred long after his death. Nostradamus's prophecies were written as short poems, called quatrains. The following are said to foretell recent events:

One burned, not dead, but apoplectical,
Shall be found to have eaten up his hands,
When the city shall damn the heretical man,
Who as they thought had changed their laws.

To the great empire, quite another shall come,
Being distant from goodness and happiness,
Governed by one of base parentage,
The kingdom shall fall, a great unhappiness.

A prominent Nostradamus scholar gives the following interpretations. The first quatrain refers to President Nixon's downfall and the Watergate scandal. The second is said to predict the rise and dominance of communism and the subsequent subjugation of the Western democracies.[10]

32. From a flyer headed "Does Sunday School Make a Difference?":

> Max Juken lived in New York. He did not believe in religious training. He refused to take his children to church, even when they asked to go. He has had 1,062 descendants; 300 were sent to prison for an average term of 13 years; 190 were prostitutes; 680 were admitted alcoholics. His family, thus far, has cost the state in excess of $420,000. They made no contribution to society.
>
> Jonathan Edwards lived in the same state, at the same time as the Jukens. He saw that his children were in church every Sunday. He had 929 descendants, of these 430 were ministers; 86 became college professors; 13 became university presidents; 75 authored good books; five were elected to the United States Congress, and two to the Senate. One was Vice-President of his nation. His family never cost the state one cent, but has contributed to the life of plenty in this land today.

33. Archeologists claim that the ancestors of American Indians made their way to the New World via a land connection across the Bering Sea. Now, anthropologist Jeffrey Goodman disputes this land-bridge hypothesis. A migration across the northernmost land would have been such an important event in their history, Goodman says, that American Indian mythology about their origins would refer to a great journey. This myth does not exist. "Conspicuously missing in all the known myths are any stories that bear the slightest resemblance to the notion of a Bering route; none seem to describe an arduous journey from Asia across the ice and snow of the north."

34. Historical records suggest that at the time of Jesus Christ, a number of individuals claimed to be the Messiah, the begotten son of God. Yet, curiously, only Jesus was able to document his claim to this title by performing miracles. No doubt, Jesus was something more than an ordinary human being. But where biblical scholars go wrong is in their assumption that Jesus was an extraordinary human being. In fact, Jesus of Nazareth was an astronaut from a civilization residing on a planet orbiting a star at great distance from our sun. Think, for a moment, of the miracles Jesus performed: healing the sick, restoring sight to the blind, reviving the recently dead, walking on water, changing water to wine. Even by the standards of modern science, it is reasonable to suppose that, given predictable advances in science and technology, such "miracles" will eventually be within our grasp. Already, modern medical science has learned how to restore the sight of the blind and to revive people long after their hearts have stopped beating. Thus, the fact that Jesus was able to perform such miracles only serves to confirm that he was a visitor to earth, able to do things that, though extraordinary and miraculous when judged by the technology of the time, were really nothing more than the product of an advanced, extraterrestrial technology.

35. Some dentists and "alternative" medical practitioners believe we are being poisoned by mercury contained in our dental fillings. When we chew, minute quantities of mercury are released from our fillings and are ingested into our bodies. Over time, the amount of mercury in the body is liable to reach toxic proportions. A flyer on mercury toxicity and dental fillings lists the following as symptoms related to mercury poisoning and suggests that if you have more than a few of these symptoms, you ought to carefully consider having your mercury amalgam fillings removed:

Anxiety	Apathy
Confusion	Depression
Emotional instability	Fits of anger
Irritability	Nervousness
Nightmares	Tension
High blood pressure	Low blood pressure
Chronic headaches	Dizziness
Muscle twitches	Ringing in ears
Cold hands or feet	Decreased sexual activity
Leg cramps	Pain in joints
Weight loss	Fatigue
Drowsiness	Lack of energy
Allergies	Oversleeping
Bad breath	Bleeding gums
Acne	Rough skin
Skin flushes	Unexplained skin rashes

A Solution to Exercise 1

The suggestion in this passage is that there is some sort of causal connection between an interest in science and an interest in music. The facts about Einstein and Newton are most likely meant to imply a correlation between the two, although the passage does not directly state that more scientists than nonscientists are interested in music. Otherwise, there would be no reason to believe that a child's interest in music would lead him or her to pursue a career in science rather than something else. Now, even if such a correlation could be established, serious questions could be raised about its significance. There are a number of ways of explaining such a correlation short of suggesting that an interest in music causes one to become interested in a career in science.

The real problem with the passage, however, is that it involves the fallacy we have called omitting facts. We are told of two instances in which well-known scientists have shown an interest in music. The crucial facts omitted, of course, are those about scientists generally. Do we have any reason to believe that what we learn about Einstein and Newton are true of scientists generally or of more scientists than nonscientists? Without this information, the causal claim made in the passage is wholly unfounded.

Notes

1. This is not to say that mainstream scientists do not, on occasion, engage in fallacious reasoning and even worse. For more on this topic, see *Betrayers of Truth: Fraud and Deceit in Science,* by William Broad and Nicholas Wade (Oxford. Oxford University Press, 1982).
2. For a detailed explanation of curious events in the Bermuda triangle, see *The Bermuda Triangle Mystery—Solved,* by Lawrence Kusche (New York: Warner Books, 1975).
3. Raymond A. Moody, *Life After Life* (New York: Bantam Books, 1975), pp. 21–22.
4. Have I violated Occam's razor in claiming that invisible imps are as likely, all things being equal, as telepathy? Perhaps. But then again perhaps not. Are there good reasons to suppose that telepathy is any less bizarre than invisible imps?
5. P. B. Medawar, *The Limits of Science* (New York: Harper & Row, 1984), p. 87.
6. Donald Rivers, "First Photo of a Human Soul," *Weekly World News,* Sept. 15, 1992. Reprinted by permission of the publisher.
7. Bernard Gittelson, *Bio-Rhythm: A Personal Science* (New York: Warner Books, 1975), pp. 15–19.
8. John Hayes, "Ex-OSU Professor Theorizes About Alien Beings," *The Oregonian,* Jan. 18, 1987. Reprinted by permission of the author.
9. Copyright © 1989 by The New York Times Company. Reprinted by permission.
10. Adapted from *The Complete Prophecies of Nostradamus,* translated, edited, and interpreted by Henry C. Roberts (New York: Nostradamus Company, 1982).

Further Reading

Scientific Method and the Philosophy of Science

Elster, Jon. *Nuts and Bolts for the Social Sciences.* Cambridge: Cambridge University Press, 1989.

Giere, Ronald N. *Understanding Scientific Reasoning.* 3rd ed. New York: Holt, Rinehart & Winston, 1991.

Hacking, Ian. *Representing and Intervening: Introductory Topics in the Philosophy of Natural Science.* Cambridge: Cambridge University Press, 1983.

Hempel, Carl G. *The Philosophy of Natural Science.* Englewood Cliffs, NJ: Prentice-Hall, 1966.

Homans, George C. *The Nature of a Social Science.* New York: Harcourt, Brace & World, 1967.

Huck, Schuyler W., and Sandler, Howard M. *Rival Hypotheses: Alternative Interpretations of Data Based Conclusions.* New York: Harper & Row, 1979.

Kuhn, Thomas S. *The Structure of Scientific Revolutions.* 2nd ed. Chicago: University of Chicago Press, 1970.

Medawar, P. B. *The Limits of Science.* New York: Harper & Row, 1984.

Moore, Kathleen Dean. *A Field Guide to Inductive Arguments.* 2nd ed. Dubuque: Kendall/Hunt, 1989.

Popper, Karl R. *The Logic of Scientific Discovery.* 2nd rev. ed. New York: Harper Torchbooks, 1968.

Salmon, Merrilee H., et al. *Introduction to the Philosophy of Science.* Englewood Cliffs, NJ: Prentice-Hall, 1992.

Toulmin, Stephen. *The Philosophy of Science: An Introduction.* New York: Harper & Row, 1960.

Pseudoscience

Abell, G. O., and Singer, B. *Science and the Paranormal.* New York: Charles Scribner's, 1981.

Broad, William, and Wade, Nicholas. *Betrayers of the Truth: Fraud and Deceit in Science.* Oxford: Oxford University Press, 1982.

Gardner, Martin. *Fads and Fallacies in the Name of Science.* New York: Dover Publications, 1957.

———. *Science: Good, Bad and Bogus.* Buffalo: Prometheus, 1981.

Glymour, Clark, and Stalker, Douglas. *Examining Holistic Medicine.* Buffalo: Prometheus, 1985.

Gray, William D. *Thinking Critically about the New Age.* Belmont, CA: Wadsworth, 1991.

Hines, Terence. *Pseudo-science and the Paranormal.* Buffalo: Prometheus, 1988.

National Council Against Health Fraud Newsletter, Box 1276, Loma Linda, CA 92354.

Radner, Daisie, and Radner, Michael. *Science and Unreason.* Belmont, CA: Wadsworth, 1982.

Randi, James. *Flim-Flam! The Truth about Unicorns, Parapsychology and Other Delusions.* New York: Thomas Y. Crowell, 1980.

Shultz, Ted, ed. *The Fringes of Reason: A Whole Earth Catalogue.* New York: Harmony Books, 1989.

The Skeptical Enquirer, Box 229, Buffalo, NY 14215-0229.

Index